THE WELLNESS LIFE-STYLE

This new series is designed to meet the growing demand for current, accessible information about the increasingly popular wellness approach to personal health. The result of a collaborative effort by a highly professional writing, editorial, and publishing team, the *Wellness* series consists of 16 volumes, each on a single topic. Each volume in this attractively produced series combines original material with carefully selected readings, relevant statistical data, and illustrations. The series objectives are to increase awareness of the value of a wellness approach to personal health and to help the reader become a more informed consumer of health-related information. Employing a critical thinking approach, each volume includes a variety of assessment tools, discusses basic concepts, suggests key questions, and provides the reader with a list of resources for further exploration.

James K. Jackson	Wellness: AIDS, STD, & Other Communicable Diseases
Richard G. Schlaadt	Wellness: Alcohol Use & Abuse
Richard G. Schlaadt	Wellness: Drugs, Society, & Behavior
Robert E. Kime	Wellness: Environment & Health
Gary Klug & Janice Lettunich	Wellness: Exercise & Physical Fitness
James D. Porterfield & Richard St. Pierre	Wellness: Healthful Aging
Robert E. Kime	Wellness: The Informed Health Consumer
Paula F. Ciesielski	Wellness: Major Chronic Diseases
Robert E. Kime	Wellness: Mental Health
Judith S. Hurley	Wellness: Nutrition & Health
Robert E. Kime	Wellness: Pregnancy, Childbirth, & Parenting
David C. Lawson	Wellness: Safety & Accident Prevention
Randall R. Cottrell	Wellness: Stress Management
Richard G. Schlaadt	Wellness: Tobacco & Health
Randall R. Cottrell	Wellness: Weight Control
Judith S. Hurley & Richard G. Schlaadt	Wellness: The Wellness Life-Style

THE WELLNESS LIFE-STYLE

Judith S. Hurley
Richard G. Schlaadt

WELLNESS

A MODERN
LIFE-STYLE
LIBRARY

The Dushkin Publishing Group, Inc./Sluice Dock, Guilford, CT 06437

To Maria

Library of Congress Catalog Card Number: 91–071810
Manufactured in the United States of America
First Edition, First Printing
ISBN: 0-87967-879-8

Library of Congress Cataloging-in-Publication Data

Hurley, Judith S. and Richard G. Schlaadt, The Wellness Life-Style
(Wellness)
     1. Health. 2. Diseases—Prevention. I. Schlaadt, Richard G. II. Title.
III. Series.
RA773   613   91–071810   ISBN 0–87967–879–8

Please see page 146 for credits

The procedures and explanations given in this publication are based on
research and consultation with medical and nursing authorities. To the best
of our knowledge, these procedures and explanations reflect currently
accepted medical practice; nevertheless, they cannot be considered absolute
and universal recommendations. For individual application, treatment
suggestions must be considered in light of the individual's health, subject to
a doctor's specific recommendations. The authors and the publisher disclaim
responsibility for any adverse effects resulting directly or indirectly from the
suggested procedures, from any undetected errors, or from the reader's
misunderstanding of the text.

JUDITH S. HURLEY

Judith S. Hurley, M.S., R.D., is a nutrition and health consultant. She was formerly Director of Employee Health Promotion for New Mexico State Government, health consultant to Los Alamos National Laboratory, a clinical nutritionist, and an instructor of nutrition at the University of Oregon. She currently consults on an international nutrition project of the U.S. National Cancer Institute and provides health promotion planning, nutrition education, and employee wellness programs to government agencies and corporations.

RICHARD G. SCHLAADT

Richard G. Schlaadt was awarded his doctorate in education from Oregon State University. He has been at the University of Oregon for 24 years, 12 years as the head of the Department of School and Community Health, prior to his current appointment as Director of the University of Oregon Substance Abuse Prevention Program. He has been active in the health education area as an officer in several health organizations and the author of over 50 professional journal articles and 5 textbooks. Dr. Schlaadt sees the *Wellness Series* as the culmination of a career's work.

WELLNESS:
A Modern Life-Style Library

General Editors
Robert E. Kime, Ph.D.
Richard G. Schlaadt, Ed.D.

Authors
Paula F. Ciesielski, M.D.
Randall R. Cottrell, Ed.D.
Judith S. Hurley, M.S., R.D.
James K. Jackson, M.D.
Robert E. Kime, Ph.D.
Gary A. Klug, Ph.D.
David C. Lawson, Ph.D.
Janice Lettunich, M.S.
James D. Porterfield
Richard St. Pierre, Ph.D.
Richard G. Schlaadt, Ed.D.

Developmental Staff
Irving Rockwood, Program Manager
Paula Edelson, Series Editor
James D. Porterfield, Developmental Editor
Wendy Connal, Administrative Assistant
Jason J. Marchi, Editorial Assistant

Editing Staff
John S. L. Holland, Managing Editor
Elizabeth Jewell, Copy Editor
Diane Barker, Editorial Assistant
Mary L. Strieff, Art Editor
Robert Reynolds, Illustrator

Production and Design Staff
Brenda S. Filley, Production Manager
Whit Vye, Cover Design and Logo
Jeremiah B. Lighter, Text Design
Libra Ann Cusack, Typesetting Supervisor
Charles Vitelli, Designer
Meredith Scheld, Graphics Assistant
Steve Shumaker, Graphics Assistant
Juliana Arbo, Typesetter
Richard Tietjen, Editorial Systems Analyst

Preface

IN RECENT YEARS, it has become clear that the way we live can be hazardous to our health. Lack of exercise, poor eating habits, and high levels of unmanaged stress are but a few of the life-style factors that influence heart disease, cancer, stroke, and stress-related illnesses. It is also apparent that the way we live determines how well (or ill) we feel, not just in the long run, but on a daily basis. Life-style patterns influence mental state, energy level, sleep, and other aspects of ourselves that determine how we feel every day.

No one can make life-style changes for us—there is no doctor, pill, or injection that will do the job. But small, simple changes, made easily and maintained over weeks, months, and years, add up to considerable benefits both now and in the future. There is a burgeoning marketplace of health and fitness products and information around us that can make it seem that one needs special equipment, clothing, or foods in order to maintain good health. In truth, one needs only a bit of motivation and some basic information.

This book provides this basic information on life-style habits that affect health and well-being. In keeping with a wellness approach, the primary focus is on topics such as the prevention of illness, fitness, nutrition, stress management, and community health. A number of self-assessments are included to help make it easier to apply this information to one's daily life. Whenever appropriate, practical guidelines are also provided.

As we move through the last decade of the century, the impact of our personal living habits, not just on our immediate health, but on the environment, is sadly apparent. Our individual well-being is inextricably linked to the health of the environment in which we live—to the health of the air, water, soil, forests, flora, and fauna. It has become critically important to use some of the effort we might put toward personal health toward community and global health. By becoming more aware of our own consumption habits, and then seeking more environmentally enlightened ways to live on our planet, we will perhaps be taking the most important health-promoting steps of all.

This is not a definitive work, but rather a place to begin. The central objective of this book is not to make you into an instant expert but to help you learn to *think critically* about the health-related claims and counterclaims with which all of us are bombarded daily. Only then will you be able to distinguish wellness fact from myth, and only then will you be an informed health consumer.

Acknowledgements

Thanks are due several people who kindly assisted with the development of this book. We especially thank Dr. Alex Waigandt of the University of Missouri for his careful review of the manuscript and many helpful suggestions. Maria Romero Facey of the New Mexico Health Promotion Bureau graciously provided advice and numerous resource materials. The editorial staff at The Dushkin Publishing Group has been superb at providing support and assistance. In particular, we extend thanks and appreciation to Irving Rockwood, Paula Edelson, Wendy Connal, and Jason J. Marchi.

Judith S. Hurley, M.S., R.D.
Richard G. Schlaadt, Ed.D.

Contents

1

The Wellness Revolution

2

How We Live, How We Die

3

The Life-Style Diseases

4

Healthy Life-Style

Page 51

FIGURES

TABLES

The Wellness Revolution

You, the individual, can do more for your own health than can any doctor, any hospital, any drug, and any exotic device. [1]

IN EVER GROWING NUMBERS, Americans are attempting to walk, jog, bicycle, swim, eat, and diet their way to health. Cholesterol levels are pondered over morning bowls of oat bran, body weights are anxiously monitored to within a few tenths of pounds, and **health spa** vacations are planned. Communities large and small sponsor competitive runs and bike races. Health and fitness magazines contain the latest advice. Companies offer comprehensive wellness programs to employees. Stress management seminars and stop smoking programs are widely available. Diet and fitness books frequently appear on the top ten bestsellers' list.

During one recent year, 1988, Americans spent more than $6 billion on athletic shoes, $74 billion on low-calorie diet foods, $5 billion on health-club memberships, $738 million on exercise equipment, $1.5 billion on bottled water, and $2.1 billion on vitamin and mineral supplements. [2]

Not everyone thinks Americans need to try so hard to stay healthy. Some experts consider us a nation of worrywarts. Rather than making us feel better and happier, they say, our pursuit of health has made us anxious to the point of feeling unwell when we are actually well and to be haunted by the possibility of future illness. [3] Many people probably spend more time worrying about their health than they spend taking the steps to improve it. Accord-

Health spa: An often luxurious, residential, resort-like facility operated on a commercial basis that offers a variety of health-related services including weight-reduction programs.

1

Table 1.1 Our Top 10 Health Concerns

1. Staying free of disease	55%
2. Avoiding smoking	55%
3. Living in an environment with clean air and clean water	47%
4. Having someone to love	44%
5. Having a positive outlook on life	44%
6. Having friends and family who are there for me when I need them	41%
7. Knowing how to cope with medical emergencies	37%
8. Avoiding excess—such as eating or drinking too much	35%
9. Eating a nutritious, balanced diet	34%
10. Getting regular exercise	33%

Source: *American Health*, March 1989, p. 67.

Many Americans are increasingly aware of the impact of life-style on health. Shown here are the percentages of those responding to a recent Yankelovich survey who indicated the item involved is "extremely important to health."

ing to market researchers, 49 percent of those who buy running shoes don't really run, 50 percent of those who buy tennis shoes don't play tennis, and 43 percent of those who buy exercise leotards never work out! [4]

People agonize about their weight but use the power lawn mower, circle parking lots searching for the spot closest to their destination, and choose the elevator instead of the stairs. Americans have added more vegetables to their diets and cut back on the consumption of fatty meats recently but eat more high-fat gourmet ice cream after dinner. [5] Women are worried about a low calcium intake, but 36 percent report they are cutting out traditional dairy foods because of concerns about fat and cholesterol. [6] Americans tell pollsters they are eating less chocolate, but sales of premium chocolate cookies increased from 55 million to 75 million pounds between 1985 and 1987. While over half of Americans report they are on a diet, consumption of high-fat snack chips has risen 60 percent since 1983. [7]

Others view the health and fitness boom with cynicism and humor. As a tongue-in-cheek response to the fitness "craze," card-carrying members of the national Couch Potatoes Club offer in their cookbook such high-fat delectables as hot dogs stuffed with cheese spread. While snacking in front of the television, one can

FIGURE 1.1
The Life-Style of a Couch Potato

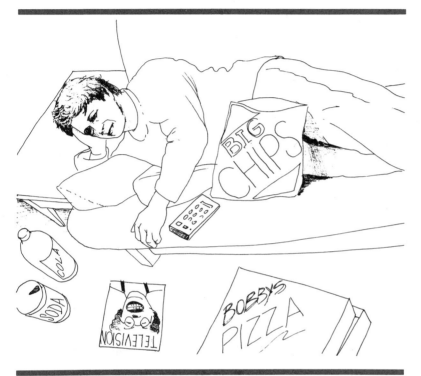

Although millions of Americans are concerned with their health and life-style, many can be found in front of the television eating high-calorie and high-fat foods.

stay warm in a couch potato sack – a goosedown cocoon sold by a mail-order company. It seems, as a nation, we are a bundle of contradictions when it comes to our health.

Is all the concern about health and fitness making us healthier and more fit? Can certain diseases be prevented by changing one's **life-style**? Can one's state of health and well-being be improved without relying exclusively on the medical profession? These questions have fueled a two-decade-long explosion in health and fitness information, products, and life-style changes in the United States.

In the movie *Sleeper,* Woody Allen wakes up to find himself in a future where doctors extol the health benefits of hot fudge sundaes and thick steaks. As we move toward the next century,

Life-style: A style of living that consistently reflects a particular set of values and attitudes.

lizabeth Blackwell, the first woman to become a doctor of medicine, was graduated from Geneva Medical College of western New York in 1849.

Table 1.2 What We're Least Satisfied With

Percentage saying they're *not* "very satisfied" with their ability to accomplish the following:

Having fewer worries in my life	80%
Managing to do everything I have to without fraying my nerves	78%
Avoiding food additives and other artificial chemicals in food	78%
Having enough time for leisure and recreation	75%
Living in an environment with clean air and clean water	73%

Source: *American Health,* March 1989, p. 67.

While most Americans are increasingly concerned about their health, many feel frustrated in their attempts to achieve their health goals.

that scenario appears, alas, unlikely. However, many feel that a little less steak and a little more exercise is not such a bad reality either–not when the benefits include less illness and disease, a longer life, and feeling better along the way. Most of us stand to gain considerably by taking better care of ourselves, eating enjoyably but wisely, turning off the television, getting off the couch, and putting to good use those exercise shoes hidden in the closet.

MEDICINE, DOCTORS, AND HEALTH

Life would be so simple if we could rely on doctors to keep us healthy, but the truth is, we can't. In spite of potent drugs and high-technology treatments, the accomplishments of medicine in the last century are often exaggerated in people's minds, and our reliance on medicine to cure us is often misplaced.

In the United States, health has improved greatly in the last 100 years when measured by how long we live. Since 1900, life expectancy has increased from an average of 47 years to the current 75 years. The statistically short **life expectancy** in 1900 was due to the large number of infant deaths caused by pneumonia-diarrhea complex, premature birth, and to a lesser extent, infectious diseases such as whooping cough, measles, and tuberculosis. [8] People who survived childhood, however, had nearly the same life expectancy that we have now–about 70 years. [9]

Life expectancy: The estimated number of years of life remaining to a living organism, usually determined by comparing the organism's current age to the average age at death of other members of the species during some fixed period.

Table 1.3 Infant Death Rates and Life Expectancy Figures for Selected Countries

Country	Infant Death Rate (Per 1,000)	Life Expectancy		
		Male	Female	Average
1. Japan	6.0	74.5	80.2	77.4
2. Sweden	6.7	73.8	79.9	76.9
3. France	8.0	70.4	78.6	74.5
4. Canada	8.5	71.9	78.9	75.4
5. Australia	9.2	72.6	79.1	75.8
6. China (Hong Kong)	9.2	72.5	78.4	75.5
7. England and Wales	9.5	71.6	77.6	74.6
8. United States	10.5	71.1	78.3	74.7
9. Israel	12.8	73.1	76.6	74.9
10. U.S.S.R.	27.7	64.0	74.0	69.0

Source: *Demographic Yearbook, 1985* (New York: Department of Economic and Social Affairs Statistical Office, United Nations, 1987), pp. 144–148.

Although the United States spends more per capita on health care than any other nation, U.S. infant mortality rates and life expectancy figures are surpassed by those of several other industrialized countries.

From the late 1800s through the 1940s, the rates of infectious disease and infant death steadily improved as beneficial changes took place in hygiene, sanitation, crowded housing conditions, water quality, and nutrition—public health, rather than medical advances. Our increased life expectancy is often attributed to advances in medicine, but antibiotics, the "wonder drugs," only appeared on the scene in the 1940s and 1950s—after rates of infectious disease had been steadily decreasing for nearly 100 years. [10]

By 1950, with major environmental improvements accomplished and infectious disease largely controlled, the formerly decreasing death rates came to a standstill—even though at the same time many medical "advances" were introduced: hospital intensive-care units, coronary-care units, open-heart surgery, organ transplants, and other high-technology modes of treatment.

(continued on p. 7)

FIGURE 1.2
The Spectre in Our Streets

Source: Bettmann Archive.

The "Spectre" was disease and death that arose from the garbage-infested streets of New York City. This 1880s cartoon condemns the unsanitary conditions that existed at the time.

Table 1.4 U.S. Life Expectancy at Birth, 1900–1989

	Males	Females	Both Sexes
Whites			
1989*	72.6	79.1	75.9
1950	66.5	72.2	69.4
1900	46.6	48.7	47.6
Blacks			
1989*	65.2	74.0	69.6
1950	58.9	62.7	60.8
1900	32.5	33.5	33.0
All Races			
1989*	71.8	78.5	75.2
1950	65.5	71.1	68.3
1900	46.3	48.3	47.3

*Provisional data; subject to change.

Source: U.S. Census Bureau, National Center for Health Statistics, 1990.

Life expectancy at birth has increased dramatically in the United States since 1900, as the above figures indicate.

Life expectancy and death rates, however, improved very little for the next 25 years in spite of the availability of the new medical treatments. [11]

After the 1950s, life-style became the next crucial factor in preventing disease. With more people now surviving into adulthood, rates of the chronic, **degenerative diseases** increased— heart disease, cancer, **diabetes**, and **stroke**. These are the diseases medicine has had little success in treating and that are most likely to develop when life-style habits are unhealthy.

The health promotion experts say it is hard for people to accept the reality that environment, nutritional state, and life-style have a greater effect on disease rates than medical treatment. Although treatment and management are available for many infirmities, medical cures exist for relatively few. The last 50 years of medical research have produced an enormous number of drugs that aid many disorders, but few inroads have been made in curing the most common ailments and diseases: heart disease, stroke, cancer, diabetes, and the common cold.

For example, in spite of new surgical treatments and drugs,

Degenerative diseases: A general category encompassing a wide range of disorders involving progressive deterioration of the structure or ability to function of some portion of the body.

Diabetes: A disorder characterized by abnormally high levels of glucose (sugar) in the blood resulting from the failure of the pancreas to produce a sufficient supply of insulin, the hormone responsible for the conversion of glucose into a form usable by the cells of the body.

Stroke: Damage to part of the brain caused by interruption in its blood supply, resulting in physical or mental impairment or even death.

Table 1.5 Infant Death Rates, New York City, per 1,000 Live Births

	1900	1930
Pneumonia-diarrhea complex	71	18
"Name" infections (including measles, tuber- culosis, whooping cough, and **erysipelas)**	14	6
Premature birth, injury at birth	30	12
Congenital malformations	6	6
All other causes	15	2

Source: Donald M. Vickery, M.D., *Life Plan for Your Health* (Reading, MA: Addison-Wesley Publishing Co., 1978), p. 20.

The pronounced decline in infant mortality that occurred in this century is often attributed to the discovery of antibiotics. However, as this table suggests, infant deaths from communicable disease had already declined dramatically before antibiotics became widely available in the late 1930s and early 1940s.

death rates for breast cancer have remained unchanged for the last 75 years. High-technology coronary-care units, regarded in the United States as crucial to recovery from a heart attack, are used less often in Great Britain, where studies show patients do just as well at home–without all the technological monitoring, away from the noise and stressful routines of a hospital stay, and for a far lower cost. [12] On the other hand, the heart-disease rate in the United States has gone down 25 percent in recent years. Health analysts attribute this change more to life-style–to an increase in exercise and a decrease in fat consumption by the population–than to medical improvements. [13]

Nevertheless, according to a study conducted by the University of Chicago, most adults believe that modern medicine has cures for nearly all diseases or will within their lifetimes. [14] Perhaps we expect too much from medicine. Considering the prevalence in our society of alcohol, cigarette, and drug use; unbalanced, high-fat diets; and lack of exercise–all habits that contribute to disease risk–one physician expresses the bare-bones reality this way: "Medical care cannot undo what you've done to yourself." [15]

THE WELLNESS CONCEPT

After the environment in which one lives and the genes with which one is born, everyday choices in life-style are the greatest

Erysipelas: An infectious disorder of the face occurring primarily among children and the elderly that produces itchy red patches on the cheeks and nose followed by pimples that blister and then crust over; it is caused by streptococcal bacteria.

FIGURE 1.3
The Decline in Death Rate, United States 1875–1975

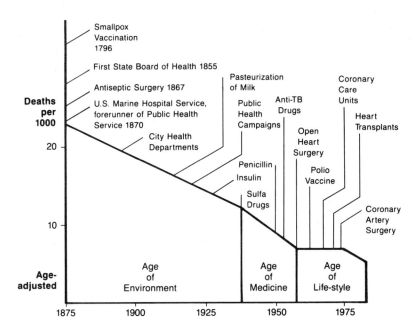

Source: Donald M. Vickery, M.D., *Lifeplan* (Reston, VA: Vicktor, Inc., 1990), p. 23.

Over 75 percent of the decline in the death rate in the United States occurred before most of modern medicine's significant discoveries became available.

determinant of health—including what we choose to eat, how much physical activity we engage in, how well we cope with stress, how safety-conscious we are, and how we use or don't use alcohol, drugs, and cigarettes.

HOLISTIC HEALTH AND WELLNESS

Health is often defined in medical terms as the absence of disease, but the word itself is derived from an Anglo-Saxon root meaning "wholeness." Wholeness implies something perfect, intact, balanced—a concept different from simply a state in which

Table 1.6 The Changing Causes of Death in the United States

The Ten Leading Causes of Death in 1900	The Ten Leading Causes of Death in 1988
1. Influenza and pneumonia	1. Heart disease
2. Tuberculosis	2. Cancer
3. Stomach and intestinal disease	3. Cerebrovascular diseases
4. Heart disease	4. Accidents
5. Cerebral hemorrhage	5. Lung disease (noncancerous)
6. Kidney disease	6. Influenza and pneumonia
7. Accidents	7. Diabetes
8. Cancer	8. Suicide
9. Diseases of early infancy	9. Cirrhosis and related liver disease
10. Diphtheria	10. Artery disease

Source: Information for 1900 is from William C. Cockerham, *Medical Sociology* 2d Edition (Englewood Cliffs, NJ: Prentice Hall, 1986), p. 24; information for 1988 is from *Mortality and Morbidity Weekly Report,* Centers for Disease Control, Atlanta, GA.

Holistic health: A view of health that encompasses the physiological, mental, emotional, social, spiritual, and environmental aspects of individuals and communities.

Wellness: An approach to personal health that emphasizes individual responsibility for well-being through the practice of health-promoting life-style behaviors.

there is no disease or illness present. In recent years, the terms **holistic health** and **wellness** have been used to describe and talk about health in a broader sense than the medical definition. Wellness has come to mean the process of moving toward *optimal* health, a state of complete physical, mental, and social well-being and not merely the absence of disease or infirmity.

Wellness, then, includes much more than just physical health. It addresses the mental, emotional, and spiritual aspects of living, as well as the relationship between these, between the individual and others, and between the individual and the larger community and environment.

The "Wellness" continuum in figure 1.4 helps delineate the difference between a medical concept of health and a wellness concept. Most of the time, most people find themselves at the neutral point of the continuum. When signs or symptoms of illness appear, treatment is generally sought, which alleviates the symptoms or the underlying illness, and one returns to the neutral point. To reach optimal health, however, one must move beyond the neutral point to the wellness side of the continuum. Through increased awareness and changes in behavior, a higher degree of health is attained than merely the absence of illness.

Moving from a state of illness or disease back to the neutral point is often achieved with the aid of medical care. If we have

The following statistics from the Metropolitan Life Insurance Company should give you added impetus to keep yourself healthy—you may have to live with the ill effects of bad health habits for a long time.

  • The number of 100-year-olds is rising so rapidly that projections by the Bureau of Census show that by the year 2000 there will be about 100,000 people aged 100 or older. And by 2050 there are expected to be about one million centenarians, a 40-fold increase over today's total.

Take Care of Yourself—You May Live to Be 100

  • Analysis of the 1979–81 life tables indicates that 1,150 Americans in 100,000 are likely to reach their hundredth birthday. (Women have markedly better chances of reaching 100 than men: 1,927 per 100,000 versus 423, according to these tables.) At the turn of the century just 31 people in 100,000 reached that milestone.

Source: *University of California Berkeley Wellness Letter,* Vol. 3, No. 6, March 1987, p. 1.

Did You Know That . . .

The 4 components of maintaining good health are proper nutrition, regular exercise, effective stress management, and routine medical checkups.

strep throat, we go to a doctor, who takes a throat culture, diagnoses the malady, and prescribes antibiotics. The wellness side of the continuum, however, includes prevention—making one's body more resistant to illness through beneficial life-style behaviors. Moving upward from the neutral point to a state of wellness can only be achieved by making positive changes in life-style. For example, a physician cannot make your heart more fit; he or she can only treat you once a heart attack or other symptom of heart disease has occurred. But *you* can incorporate a brisk walk into your day and eat fewer fatty foods to help prevent heart disease and the need for medical care later on. A physician cannot take away your fatigue (unless it is related to a specific medical condition), but *you* can choose to eat the foods and engage in the kinds of physical activities that help you feel fit and full of energy.

Wellness is not a static state, but a process in which the individual continually makes choices, takes action, moves, and grows—an approach that returns the concept of health to its root meaning, that of balance and wholeness, and puts it in the hands of the individual, not the health-care system. No single choice during the day necessarily determines health, but rather the balance of all the decisions made day in and day out.

One begins the process from wherever one is on the contin-

Did You Know That . . .

Ralph Waldo Emerson said, "The first wealth is health."

Wellness Is

knowing what your real needs are and how to get them met;

expressing emotions in ways that communicate what you are experiencing to other people;

acting assertively, and not passively or aggressively;

enjoying your body by means of adequate nutrition, exercise, and physical awareness;

being engaged in projects that are meaningful to you and reflect your most important inner values;

knowing how to create and cultivate close relationships with others;

responding to challenges in life as opportunities to grow in strength and maturity, rather than feeling beset by "problems";

creating the life you really want, rather than just reacting to what "seems to happen";

relating to troublesome physical symptoms in ways that bring improvement in condition as well as increased knowledge about yourself;

enjoying a basic sense of well-being, even through times of adversity;

knowing your own inner patterns—emotional and physical—and understanding "signals" your body gives you;

trusting that your own personal resources are your greatest strength for living and growing;

experiencing yourself as a Wonderful Person.

—*John Travis, M.D.*

Source: John W. Travis, M.D., *Wellness Workbook* (Mill Valley, CA: Wellness Research Center, 1977, 1981, 1988).

uum, in whatever current state of health, physical limitation, or illness. The choices that improve health will be unique to each individual. As daily choices in behavior are made, some will be negative—potentially moving one down the continuum—and some positive, moving one up the continuum. By gradually choosing more of the positive life-style behaviors, each individual's optimal state of wellness can be approached.

Health can't be purchased from a physician or the health-care system. To a large extent, we create it. This doesn't mean that when one becomes ill, as we all do at times, the individual is somehow "to blame" for allowing this to occur, nor does it mean that medical care is not appropriate. Perfect health is not attainable—periodic bouts of illness or infirmity are part of the natural

FIGURE 1.4
The Wellness Continuum

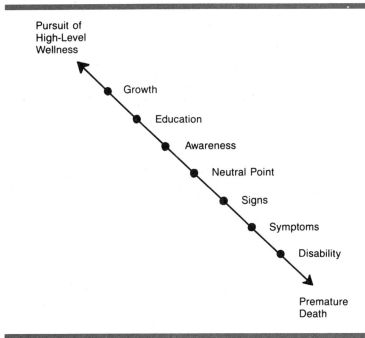

The wellness continuum is a device for visualizing the difference between a wellness conception of health and a purely medical definition.

cycle of living, growing, aging, and interacting with the environment. But whatever your current state of health or illness, you can influence and remain in charge of your health by becoming aware and knowledgeable, developing positive life-style patterns, and being actively involved in medical treatment decisions when necessary. It is in this way we can move beyond the neutral point to a more vibrant level of well-being. "Wellness" describes this dynamic process, this path we can create—it is a lifetime both in the making and in the enjoying. W

C H A P T E R

2

How We Live, How We Die

" **C**OFFEE CAUSES CANCER," "airplanes are unsafe," "sugar is a poison," "apples are full of pesticides." Living, it seems, is risky. Overwhelmed by news reports and health warnings that make it seem danger lurks everywhere, we can be easily tempted to give up and feel nothing is worth worrying about or can become completely confused about how to sort out valid concerns from unnecessary anxieties.

People occasionally have heart attacks during exercise, so is it safer to stay **sedentary**? Since plane accidents are a possibility, is it less risky to drive? Is it better to avoid fruit with its pesticide residues that might cause cancer . . . or to eat fruit for its nutrients and fiber that protect against cancer? Is our anxiety harming our health more than the risk itself?

On the other hand, rather than worry too much, people often ignore the biggest risks to health because they are "hidden." We learn at an early age to look both ways before crossing the street. If we don't, the chance of being hit by a car sooner or later is quite high. Because we can see cars whizzing by, the risk is obvious to us and we are highly motivated to be cautious. The results of other risky behaviors are often less obvious because they appear years later—but the risk is no less significant. A person who gets little exercise, eats a high-fat diet, and leads a hurried, stressful life is very likely to develop fat-clogged arteries by the time he or she reaches middle age and may suffer a heart attack. But at the time when we are deciding whether we will eat the extra serving of steak or sit in front of the television the fourth evening in a row the potential consequences seem far away, and we feel no pressure to forgo the risky behavior. This is particularly so for

Sedentary: Accustomed to sitting or being inactive.

14

True or false:

1. Eating garlic lowers blood cholesterol.

2. Alcoholism is an inherited disease.

3. Coffee causes pancreatic cancer.

4. Megadoses of B vitamins cure premenstrual syndrome.

If you based your answers on what you've read in the newspapers or heard on TV, you may accept all four statements as scientific fact. Yet the first two have never been proven, and the second two are patently false. These *propositions*—which would have obvious applications in daily life if they were proven true—have been extensively studied and publicized. How do you identify the "truth" in health news?

Health News: A Good Story or a Good Study?

"Study," once upon a time, was a verb denoting what a student did (or failed to do) before an exam, but lately there's hardly a cereal box or a magazine ad that doesn't cite some study—all too often featuring a few "stretchers," as Huckleberry Finn called them. Formerly the private turf of the medical profession, such publications as the *New England Journal of Medicine* and the *Journal of the American Medical Association* are now quoted everywhere from the evening news to the Shoppers' Special. In addition, new scientific journals have sprung up like weeds. By one estimate, nearly a quarter million biomedical articles are published in English alone each year.

Thus any piece of scientific work, no matter how insignificant, can make headlines—and because health news is such a hot topic, it usually does. This has some advantages, to be sure. It's a good sign when so many people want to know what's going on. After all, much scientific work is paid for with tax dollars. You have every right and reason to try to stay informed about your health and everything that might affect it.

Source: *University of California Berkeley Wellness Letter,* Vol. 6, No. 12, September 1990, p. 4.

Did You Know That . . .

High blood pressure, smoking, and an elevated cholesterol level increase the risk of heart attack more in middle-aged women than in men of the same age.

behaviors that do not cause problems when engaged in now and then, such as an occasional high-fat meal or a week without brisk activity, but which result in problems when done too frequently over a long period of time. It's so easy for "just this once" to become a lifetime of "usually."

RISKY BUSINESS

The conditions, situations, and behaviors that contribute to injury, illness, or death are termed **risk factors**. When something is termed a risk factor, it does not mean it causes the undesired outcome 100 percent of the time. It means that of those people who engage in the behavior or are exposed to the unsafe condition, a certain number will probably experience the undesired outcome. The riskier the behavior or condition (the stronger its known link with a negative outcome), the more likely an individual is to experience the undesired result.

Some risks we face are of our own choosing, such as driving after drinking or taking up hang-gliding. Others are involuntary or imposed on us, such as the leaching of chemicals into a community water supply from an industrial plant or having inherited genes from our parents that predispose us to high blood cholesterol. Some risks are partly voluntary and partly involuntary. For example, each individual ultimately decides whether to take up cigarette smoking, but massive efforts by advertisers and government subsidies for tobacco growers have exposed us involuntarily to an environment that exerts tremendous pressure on people to smoke.

The riskiness of various behaviors and conditions is determined in part through **epidemiological research**, which involves studying large groups of people and asking: How many people who engage in a certain behavior experience a certain outcome? For example, when we examine the dietary fat intake of people in several countries and the corresponding rates of heart disease, it is apparent that heart disease occurs significantly more often in populations with high-fat diets. This does not prove that high-fat diets cause heart disease, however. Experimental and clinical research studies on animals and humans, in which conditions are carefully set up to test a hypothesis, are often needed to confirm relationships between behaviors or conditions and illness or death. In the case of heart disease, laboratory animals fed high-fat diets develop the condition much more often than those fed low-fat diets. They also develop high blood cholesterol levels. Studies in humans show that high-fat diets lead to elevated blood cholesterol levels and that lowering blood cholesterol lowers rates of heart disease.

Over time, clearer and clearer pictures emerge about the degree of danger or risk a particular situation engenders, until health experts or scientists or someone with good observation

Risk factor: A situation or condition that contributes to the likelihood that an undesirable outcome will occur, generally established by multiple scientific studies.

Epidemiological research: The study of large populations in order to investigate the causes and control of diseases.

FIGURE 2.1
Risky Substances

Illegal drugs such as heroin, crack, and cocaine are extremely dangerous. But legal substances such as alcohol, nicotine, and prescription drugs can be just as lethal if abused.

Did You Know That . . .

It is a myth that alcohol will help you sleep better. You will fall asleep faster after 1 or 2 drinks, but your sleep is likely to be more fragmented and you are likely to wake up suddenly once the effects of the alcohol have worn off.

skills can say, "If you do this, chances are good that such and such will occur." The next step is up to us.

The Ostrich Syndrome

Even after learning that a behavior involves relatively high risk, many people continue to engage in it or remain exposed to the hazardous condition. One reason is that being healthy is not everyone's top priority, although it tends to become a priority as soon as a bout of illness or an accident occurs. There is also a tendency to think "I'm different—that problem won't happen to me," or to believe one's other attributes or practices will prevent

Risk-benefit analysis: A technique for assessing the likely outcome of a particular decision by quantifying and then comparing both the potential risks (losses) and benefits (gains).

illness or harm: "I'm a safe driver, I don't need to wear a seat belt," or "I exercise, so I don't have to bother about the fat in my diet," or "I'm young now, I've got plenty of time to cut down on alcohol before it will affect my health." People may feel that they don't know what change is appropriate or how to successfully implement such a change. Like old dogs, we are resistant to learn-

(continued on p. 22)

How Much Risk Is Too Much?

It wasn't science. Raymond Hayducka did his risk-benefit calculations over a beer in a smoke-filled Newark, N.J., taproom while a dispirited-looking stripper cracked her gum in time to the bump and grind.

Outside, moon-suited technicians from the EPA were carefully scraping up soil samples at the site of an abandoned chemical plant, looking for traces of dioxin, a chemical so toxic that health officials consider it unwise for humans to be exposed to any amount.

But Hayducka, taking an exaggerated breath and thumping his chest, said confidently, "I worked in the chemical plant for 16 years and I've never been sick. I won't waste my time worrying about it." It was a swift and simple mental calculation: The certainty of a weekly paycheck weighed against an unproved physical threat.

As an analytical technique, however, it was not much cruder than the ones government officials use daily in weighing the highly visible benefits of the chemical revolution against its pervasive—and little understood—risks.

Risk-benefit analysis has been around for years, the tool of stockbrokers, insurance companies, and speculators. But more recently it has become an increasingly important handmaiden of government regulators, applied to sensitive questions involving health and safety.

The new emphasis has opened a Pandora's box of questions, many of them revolving around the imponderables of morality, the value of human life, and the right of free men and women to accept risk versus the government's obligation to protect citizens from risks thrust upon them involuntarily.

Such risk-benefit questions have been an is-sue, for example, at the National Institute for Occupational Safety and Health (NIOSH), which conducted a 15-year study of workers and work places. NIOSH had the names of as many as 250,000 people who may face increased risk of life-threatening diseases because of exposure to toxic substances at work. But the government refused to notify the people, citing substantial cost, confusion about whether the medical dangers justify a government warning, and fear of alarming some communities. [Later] the Public Citizen Health Research Group disclosed the names of 249 work places involved, information obtained through a Freedom of Information Act request.

At its most extreme, the chemical risk was starkly evident in Bhopal, India, where a poison-gas leak from a pesticide plant killed more than 2,000 people and injured 100,000 more in a matter of hours.

Investigators have not determined whether the catastrophe in Bhopal was preventable or whether it was the kind of industrial accident that will happen under the most restrictive safety practices. But the tragedy served to sharpen debate on a broader question: How well does society understand the risks of chemicals that do not come as a suffocating cloud in the dark of night but as an invisible and inescapable part of our daily lives?

The debate is most intense inside the EPA, which has taken the lead in promoting risk-benefit analysis. Former EPA Administrator William Ruckelshaus addressed the issue squarely in one of his first speeches after returning to the agency in 1983.

"We must assume that life now takes place in a mine field of risks from hundreds, perhaps thou-

sands, of substances," Ruckelshaus told the National Academy of Sciences. "No more can we tell the public: 'You are home free with an adequate margin of safety.' "

Against the staggering size of the regulatory task, the argument has undeniable intellectual force. More than 60,000 chemicals are in commercial use in the United States, and the industry produces a thousand new ones every year. There are 35,000 or more pesticides, 8,600 food additives, and 3,400 cosmetic ingredients.

Before World War II, U.S. industry produced less than 10 billion pounds of synthetic organic chemicals each year. By 1980 the figure was 350 billion pounds and still climbing.

To grapple with a problem of that magnitude, Ruckelshaus argues, the government needs a uniform way of measuring risks and a statutory formula for balancing them against the economic value of a substance and the costs of controlling it.

"If the government gets better at both assessing and managing risk, and we do it accurately, people will have a better sense of the risks and will act sensibly," he says.

But even within the EPA, opinions are sharply divided over whether the agency can provide the kind of accuracy Ruckelshaus envisions.

"It's not a scientific process," one EPA scientist says. "Nobody faults it directly. It's really the best we can do. But when you go out for a beer after the meeting, they talk about how uncomfortable they are."

Inside the EPA, the overseer of risk is Elizabeth L. Anderson, director of the EPA's Office of Health and Environmental Assessment. Anderson is in charge of the team that does the calculations, assessing the risks of perhaps a hundred chemicals a year by selecting information, or "data points," from laboratory results and plugging them into a complex mathematical formula.

The agency considers the assessments only a tool to help regulators do their job. But risk assessment has become an increasingly important tool, one used as often to justify a decision not to regulate a pollutant as to justify regulating one. Not surprisingly, the assessments are often viewed with skepticism outside the agency.

"It's an inexact science at best, and all too often it's used as a rationale for not regulating," says Nicholas Freudenberg, a professor of public health at the City University of New York. "The fact is that there is a tremendous amount of uncertainty, and if you need certainty, even from animal tests, you're not going to have it for decades."

Like others at the EPA, Anderson harbors no illusions about the certainty of her office's product. Between the raw laboratory data and the finished product are dozens of assumptions, mathematical manipulations, and educated guesses.

"It's almost like a circumstantial murder trial," she says.

Another EPA official puts it more bluntly: "We have been accused of drawing numbers out of thin air—and that may not be a bad analogy."

Consider the variables: A hypothetical chemical is tested in a laboratory on rats and mice of strains carefully bred to be extraordinarily sensitive to cancer-causing agents.

Male mice develop tumors at a high rate, female mice at a far lower rate. Rats develop no tumors at all.

Is a rat a better forecaster of human response than a mouse? Should the chemical be regarded as a human carcinogen? And if so, how powerful?

"We don't know which laboratory animals are closest to humans, so we have to take seriously the most sensitive animal model," Anderson says.

But human exposure to any chemical rarely comes close to the deliberately high doses administered to a laboratory animal. To complete the risk assessment, the EPA's mathematical model must have some estimate of real human exposure.

In most cases, hard numbers do not exist.

"We found out at Love Canal that we could spend $10 million at one shot and still not know what people are exposed to," Anderson says.

So the agency gobbles up whatever information it can find, often subjecting the raw figures to still more mathematical conversions.

If an agricultural chemical is used on apples,

how much residue will remain on each apple? How many apples will a person eat each year? Will the residue remain if the apple is turned into juice, sauce, or pastry? If so, how much juice will be drunk, how many pastries consumed?

What eventually emerges from the estimates and calculations is nothing more than mathematics masquerading as science; even the most devout adherents of the art acknowledge that the risk figure suggests a mathematical certainty that does not exist. If a risk assessment shows a 1-in-10,000 risk of cancer from a chemical to which 500,000 people are assumed to be exposed at certain assumed levels, for example, does that mean 50 cancers will result?

Maybe. But maybe not. Because of the conservative assumptions at each step of the process, the EPA says risk assessment produces an "upper bound" value. The presumed incidence of cancer will be no higher than 50, according to the EPA, but it could be considerably lower.

"I think that we're overstating the risks very substantially," one EPA scientist says. "I still think it's appropriate. I just don't think we should kid ourselves that this is an attack on cancer."

But other EPA officials privately worry that the assessments also may offer a false sense of security. The agency knows almost nothing about the possibility of synergistic or combined effects of exposures to many chemicals, for instance, and frequently is hampered by inadequate laboratory data, which forces still more assumptions, more manipulations, more guesswork.

"The answer eventually comes back that we don't know what to make of these models," Anderson says. "Given all of this, so much gets lost. You just see these numbers, and so many bodies."

Throughout the day and night, the average American is exposed to hundreds of chemicals.

The Food and Drug Administration estimates that three fourths of all foods contain minute residues of agricultural chemicals; processing may add others, in the form of preservatives, flavorings, and colorings.

In the house there are household cleaners, insect sprays, formaldehyde fumes. Freshly dry-cleaned clothes give off the faint aroma of perchlorethylene. A trip to the self-service gasoline station means breathing a little benzene, perhaps some ethylene dichloride, a few molecules of lead.

There's saccharin in the soda pop, chloroform in the air, trihalomethanes in the water.

By statistical standards, none of those chemicals presents the risk that the average American assumes willingly by using the automobile. The risks of dying in an automobile accident in any given year are one in 5,000. Over a lifetime, the risk is far higher—about two in 100, half that if seat belts are worn.

For some other self-imposed risks, the figures are even higher. For pack-a-day cigarette smokers, the risk of cancer is one in ten.

What, by contrast, are the risks from exposure to chemicals? Individual figures are hard to come by. According to the National Academy of Sciences, for example, fewer than 10 percent of this country's agricultural chemicals and 5 percent of its food additives have been fully tested for their ability to cause chronic health problems.

But consider the case of saccharin, one of the most exhaustively studied chemical compounds. According to a 1982 Harvard University study, drinking 40 diet sodas carries with it a one-in-a-million chance of cancer.

Someone who drank a diet soda each day for 70 years, then, would face a cancer risk of 6.4 in 10,000.

By one of the most commonly cited estimates, a 1981 study by two Oxford University scientists, about 8,000 Americans may die each year of cancer linked to exposure to environmental pollutants. The EPA has estimated that the annual number of cancer deaths linked to toxic air pollutants alone could be as high as 2,000.

The Oxford study estimated another 8,000 or so cancer deaths from food additives and "industrial products," and perhaps 16,000 more from occupational exposures. By contrast, the same study estimated more than 120,000 annual cancer deaths associated with tobacco and 140,000 associated with diet.

Because a far higher proportion of deaths are attributable to tobacco and food habits, some health officials argue that the regulatory efforts on chemicals are entirely misplaced.

"If I ran the zoo" an EPA official says, "I'd outlaw smoking. You'd certainly save more lives."

But others worry that the impact of chemical exposures has yet to show up in the cancer statistics.

"When lung cancer became epidemic, it was a small proportion of total deaths," said epidemiologist Devra Lee Davis of the National Academy of Sciences. "We have no way of knowing until 40 years from now."

As Ruckelshaus tells it, the manager of a rubber-products plant had determined to level with his workers about the hazards of cancer-causing vinyl chloride and the new rules designed to limit their exposure to it.

"He went on at some length," Ruckelshaus said, "explaining the risks, and how safety rules would change, and health monitoring. At the end of the presentation, he asked if there were any questions, and there was a long silence. And I thought, boy, are they going to storm the stage or what?

"Finally, one worker piped up. He said, 'When are you gonna get this damn cigarette machine fixed?' "

Ruckelshaus tells the story to illustrate what some regulators see as the great paradox in risk regulation: The public will accept some very high and unquestionable risks, but will vehemently reject others of lesser consequence.

In truth, neither the agency nor industry has had much success in relating risk to the public through comparisons—the documented hazards of a high-fat diet, for instance, versus the less certain and presumably smaller risks of food preservatives.

"I used to think that had a lot of potential," says Ruckelshaus. "I'm not so sure anymore. They don't believe you, for one thing. . . . And it's been misused. People tend to compare everything to cigarettes, figuring that if the public accepts cigarettes as okay, then Lord, anything's okay."

Critics of risk assessment, however, find no paradox in the public reaction. Reducing all risks

to a set of finite and comparative figures, they argue, tends to obscure the fundamental difference between a voluntary risk and an involuntary one, and ignores a person's right to conduct his or her own risk-benefit analysis.

A person who drives to work daily, for example, voluntarily accepts the hazards of the automobile in return for the obvious benefit: The car transports the person to work and back.

The same person may be unwilling to accept even the smallest amount of a chemical carcinogen that makes its way into drinking water from a nearby hazardous-waste dump. Whatever the statistical risks involved, they far outweigh the nonexistent personal benefits.

A person in that position is not likely to be comforted by a regulatory calculation that finds the potential damage to human health is too low to justify the high cost of removing the chemical.

EPA officials confronted a similar reaction [in 1984] in Tacoma, Wash., where the agency conducted an unusual experiment in public education on the risks of arsenic from a copper smelter. The smelter provided a benefit to the community—several hundred jobs—but also a broadly shared risk of lung cancer from arsenic emissions that could not be totally stopped, short of closing the facility.

The EPA held extensive hearings and trotted out its "upper bound" risk assessments. The smelter hired a public relations company to help explain the economic benefits of the plant. But by the end of the arduous experiment, dozens of Tacomans were sporting buttons that said, simply, "Both."

Some scientists and public policy experts rated the effort a failure, and have suggested privately that such official candor might not be the wisest course for the EPA to pursue.

Ruckelshaus flatly rejected that notion. "We've embarked on a process in which we will involve the public in this, and we can't back away," he said. "The more they know, the more comfortable they become with the concept."

Source: *Washington Post National Weekly Edition*, 4 February 1985.

ing new tricks. It is easier to continue our usual patterns than to initiate change.

You may know someone who did everything "wrong" yet survived to a healthy, fit old age. "My grandfather smoked like a chimney and had his whiskey every day, and it didn't hurt him a bit. He lived to be 96." Should we follow grandfather's example with confidence that we too will live to a healthy, ripe old age? Probably not—such stories interest us precisely because most of us have heard that cigarettes and alcohol are bad for our health. Here is an exception, someone who may make us feel we can take the same risks and defeat the odds.

Smoking, research tells us, is clearly a risk factor for development of lung and heart disease, and alcohol use is a risk factor for accidents, alcohol dependency, liver disease and cancer. People who "smoke like a chimney" and drink to excess for much of their lives have a higher likelihood of developing some form of cancer, lung disease, or heart disease. If you smoke and drink excessively, you may be as fortunate as grandfather and live to a healthy and ripe old age, but this outcome is less likely to occur than another—that of illness and **premature death**.

Being alive means being involved in challenges, decisions, and activities that carry some degree of risk. The point in learning how to improve or maintain one's health is not to become fearful or anxious, but rather to reduce worry by developing confidence in one's ability to manage the few important behaviors that lead to a long and active life. Most hazards we commonly face are small ones, and a few are large. Assuming one's goal is a long and healthy life, it is probably more worthwhile to assess one's life-style for the big risks that can be controlled and to worry less about the rest.

There is no way to predict the consequences of any given risky behavior or condition for a specific individual, but one can estimate the odds. Whether you choose to try to beat the odds and engage in risky behavior or stack the deck in your favor by avoiding the risk is up to you.

HOW WE DIE

Premature death: Death before an individual reaches the standard life expectancy.

Trauma: Any sudden, severe, physical injury or psychological shock.

The leading cause of death in the United States is heart disease, followed by cancer, cerebrovascular disease (stroke), and accidents. Causes of premature death vary between different age groups, however. In people below age 44, **trauma** is the leading cause. In particular, among those 15 to 25 years of age, it takes an astonishingly large toll: 75 percent of deaths are caused by accidents, homicide, and suicide. [1] For those over age 44, the four leading causes of death are the same as those for the whole population combined: heart disease, followed by cancer, cerebrovascular disease, and accidents. [2]

(continued on p. 26)

Low Risk, High Risk

Taking control of your health

How would you answer the following questions:

1. You are about to plan a 1,000-mile journey, and you aren't pressed for time. Rank the following means of transportation from the safest to the riskiest: bus, train, plane, and passenger car.

2. What would you say kills more Americans annually: heart disease, cancer, or automobile accidents?

3. You're a healthy 45-year-old man, slightly overweight. Your father and his brother both died in their fifties of heart disease. Your mother, now 65, has had Type II diabetes for several years. Are you likely to get one of these ailments?

4. Winston Churchill, not to mention your Aunt Harriet, drank brandy and smoked habitually and was overweight besides. Both lived into their eighties and died peacefully in their sleep. Does that prove there's something health experts don't know?

5. You're a 43-year-old woman, a good cook, and you like a glass of wine or two with fine food. You were upset to read recently that even moderate alcohol consumption may double a woman's risk of getting breast cancer. The experts further stated that quitting now might not reduce the risk. However, you stopped drinking wine. Your sister is a teetotaler. Are you twice as likely to get breast cancer as she is?

6. You're 50, female, and a smoker. Your last checkup showed that both your blood pressure and blood cholesterol level were somewhat higher than they should be. You know this means that you risk a heart attack or stroke, but you read an article that said that even 50-year-old male smokers with high blood pressure and elevated cholesterol have only a 13% chance of getting sick within six years. So you're looking on the bright side: you've got an 87% chance of staying healthy for the next six years. Is this a constructive attitude?

Questions 1 and 2: figuring the odds

Of these questions, only the first two have fairly straightforward answers. You're safest in a bus, and in greatest danger in an automobile. (More than 10 people die per billion automobile and taxi miles; but it takes more than 2 billion bus miles to produce a fatality. Trains and planes are 10 times safer than cars, but only about half as safe as buses.) But whether they travel or stay at home, more Americans die from heart disease each year than from anything else. The purpose of the questions above, however—all of which will be discussed in the course of this article—is not so much to produce correct answers as to invite you to figure your odds.

Efforts to identify health risks—and reduce them, if possible—are as old as medicine itself. Hippocrates advised his fellow physicians to "consider the seasons of the year and what effects each of them produces" and to take note of what people drank and ate and how they lived. Scientists today are still looking for the determinants of health, albeit with a little more sophistication and scientific knowledge. Epidemiology (literally, the study of epidemics) is the attempt to identify the factors that cause diseases and injuries to determine what the probabilities are that they *will* cause them, and to determine how to decrease or eliminate the identified risk. This is often referred to as risk hazard appraisal, which is of growing importance in medical science, especially in the effort to prevent disease and promote health. Once the risk factors are known,

the next job is to make changes in the environment (for example, to persuade manufacturers to
install seat belts of a certain design) and to
persuade people to change their behavior (for
example, convince them to fasten the belt).

. . . Like a horseplayer at the race track, we're
simply quoting odds. No one can honestly assure
you that doing one thing will kill you, while re-
fraining from doing it will keep you safe. For
example, on the average, one out of ten smokers
gets lung cancer, but only a rare nonsmoker gets
it. If you are an average smoker, your chances of
getting lung cancer at any time of life are 24
times higher than those for nonsmokers, and the
risk increases as the amount of smoking increases.

Thus you're asked to draw your own conclusions. In the science of risk assessment, there's
no such thing as absolute safety, but you can
choose to widen or narrow your safety margins.
And though scientists may assess the risks, how
you manage your life is up to you. It's often hard
to evaluate what the experts say, and the press
seldom makes your task simpler. The headline
"Alcohol shown to cause breast cancer" will
attract more readers than "Study suggests alcohol intake slightly increases breast cancer risk for
some women." It is always easier to oversimplify
than to tell people how complicated things really
are.

Questions 3 and 4: heredity is not destiny

If your father died young of a heart attack, you
have a good chance of following in his footsteps.
Knowing your inherited liabilities, though, gives
you an excellent opportunity to alter them. The
genetic odds may be lowered significantly if you
are not overweight, keep your blood pressure
under control, and maintain a low blood cholesterol level. If your mother has diabetes, that's an
indication that weight control and exercise are
crucially important for you.

For many of us, familial tendencies constitute
an emotional trap. People whose parents or
grandparents died at comparatively young ages
of heart disease or cancer, or some other disease
with a genetic component, usually realize that

this heritage works against them and may falsely
conclude that taking care of their own health is
irrelevant. On the other hand, if all your relatives
were as indestructible as Winston Churchill or
the hypothetical Aunt Harriet, you may have an
equally false sense of invulnerability.

Researchers may one day unravel the genetic
code and come closer to accurately predicting your
chances of getting a disorder such as heart disease
or hypertension. But today only a few diseases are
known to have purely genetic causes, for example,
hemophilia, in which a blood-clotting factor is absent; sickle cell anemia, a blood disorder that
occurs most commonly among people of African
descent; cystic fibrosis; and certain forms of kidney
disease.

In many ailments that show signs of running in
families, such as cancer, heart disease, or diabetes, heredity is only one factor in the mix. Your
biological and cultural heritage and your environment interact, and it's the interaction that counts.
Your diet or exercise habits or your environment
may foster, or foil, the tendencies you were born
with.

Question 5: alcohol and breast cancer

[In 1987], as reported in the *New England Journal of Medicine* and subsequently in scores of
newspapers and magazines, studies by two
prestigious research groups independently demonstrated a link between alcohol intake and
breast cancer. A woman who drank even as few
as three beers or glasses of wine weekly was
found to have a 50% greater lifetime risk of
developing breast cancer than a nondrinking
woman. Widely publicized along with that figure
was another statistic: that one American woman
out of 11 develops breast cancer at some time in
her life. That's a risk of 9%. It seems logical to
conclude therefore, as many reporters did, that
women drinkers run a risk closer to 14%, a
terrifying narrowing of the safety margin.

But here's what very few of the reports made
clear: the one-in-eleven figure applies to all
American women indiscriminately, from age 1 to
85. That is, it's a lifetime average and does not
describe the odds for an individual over shorter

intervals. The incidence of breast cancer in the population rises with age. A 40-year-old woman has about a 3.3% chance of developing breast cancer by age 60. If she's a moderate drinker her chances would increase by half—to about 4.8% —if the reported studies are correct. That's a little less horrifying than 14%.

Furthermore, though the two studies considered other risk factors, they point up many problems. For example, the estimation of what the women actually ate and drank was based on poor data obtained only at the beginning of the studies, which lasted from four to ten years. The investigators did not determine the women's previous eating and drinking habits, or whether these habits changed while the studies were going on. In addition, they did not rule out the chance that something besides alcohol is increasing the cancer risk in the lives of moderate drinkers.

Then in March [1988], Dr. Susan Chu of the Centers for Disease Control in Atlanta reported that a new study of 7,000 women (based on a different approach) found no association at all between alcohol and breast cancer. Clearly, a lot more medical research needs to be done. If you're a woman wondering whether an occasional drink will do you good or harm, the answer is still up in the air: no cause and effect relationship between alcohol and breast cancer has yet been demonstrated. Heavy drinking is of course associated with many disorders. But women who drink occasionally need not berate themselves for having unwittingly shortened their lives.

Question 6: heart attack roulette

A 50-year-old smoker, male or female, with elevated blood cholesterol and blood pressure is seriously courting cardiovascular disease. You may have only a 13% chance of developing it, since neither you nor your doctor has any way of predicting whether you'll fall into the lucky 87% who do not develop heart disease or the unlucky 13% who do. If these sound like favorable odds, you may decide not to make any changes in your habits. However, a more realistic way to consider the odds is as follows. If your risk factors were low (that is, you didn't smoke and your blood pressure and blood cholesterol levels were low), your chances of having a heart attack between age 40 and 64 would be only 6%. However, if you continue to smoke and do nothing about your other risk factors, your chance of having a heart attack during these years is 40%. This is a very big difference. Giving up cigarettes, controlling your blood pressure, and lowering your blood cholesterol level would significantly widen your safety margin. Obviously, that's the constructive action to take.

Another example of this kind of reasoning can be seen in the relationship between oral contraceptives and heart attacks. High-dose oral contraceptives increase the risk of heart attack by a factor of 4.7. This sounds like a very large increase. However, if you're a 20- to 24-year-old woman, your heart attack risk is less than 1 in 500,000. Thus a fivefold increase represents only about 5 in 500,000 (or 1 in 100,000). This means that if all 8.5 million American women in this age group were to take oral contraceptives, 80 of them (instead of the expected 17) would have heart attacks. This would produce many fewer deaths than might result from unwanted pregnancies in the same age group. And even this small risk has been markedly reduced by the new low-dose estrogen contraceptives.

Risk in perspective

So be cautious in interpreting articles that talk about doubling or tripling your risk of getting a specific disease. To make sense of a twofold or threefold increase in risk, first you have to know how likely you are to get the disease anyway. For example, if your chances of developing a certain illness are 1 in 100,000, a doubled risk brings you up to 2 in 100,000 (or 1 in 50,000). Those are still pretty low odds. However, if 1 out of 10 people develops this illness and you do something that doubles your risk, your chances are now 1 in 5. That's a very significant increase.

Source: *University of California Berkeley Wellness Letter*, Vol. 4, No. 9, June 1988, pp. 4–5.

The factors that account for these premature deaths in the United States today fall into four categories: heredity, lack of basic medical care, environment, and life-style. [3] Life-style habits, the factor one has the most control over, account for over half the causes of premature death.

If we examine these behaviors more closely, particular ones clearly emerge as culprits. The most significant are smoking, being sedentary, not wearing seat belts, using alcohol, and certain dietary habits.

The extent to which life-style behaviors can promote either health or disease and injury becomes clearer when we examine the magnitude of their impact. Consider the following:

* One in 2 adults develops cardiovascular disease. [4]
* Thirty percent of adults develop cancer. [5]
* Thirty-six percent of adults have elevated blood pressure, increasing their risk for stroke. [6]
* More than half of all adults have elevated blood cholesterol. [7]
* The fat content of the typical American diet is 37 percent, not the recommended level of 30 percent or less. [8]
* Fewer than half of all adults obtain the minimum amount of physical activity known to help prevent heart disease. [9]
* Twenty to 30 percent of the population are overweight. [10]
* Each week, 350 to 500 people die in car accidents between Friday and Sunday. [11]
* Eleven percent of motorcycle crashes involve alcohol; 40 percent of the fatal ones involve alcohol. [12]
* The majority of gun deaths and injuries occur in households where a gun is kept. [13]
* One thousand cycling fatalities occur annually in the United States; head injuries to cyclists account for 85 percent of these deaths. [14]
* Each day, 3,000 young people (1 million per year) take up smoking. [15]
* The number of Americans killed each year from smoking is greater than the number of Americans killed during World War II and the Vietnam War combined. [16]

On the other hand, you may be among the Americans who have begun to make significant changes in life-style:

* Each year, 1.3 million Americans quit smoking. [17]
* Eighty-four percent of parents use car safety seats for their infants and toddlers, triple the 1981 percentage. [18]

FIGURE 2.2
Youth and Sports

The percentage of females participating in school athletic activities has increased significantly over the past 2 decades.

- Over half the runners who finished the demanding Boston Marathon in 1989 were over age 40. [19]
- Thirty-five percent of children and teenagers participating in school athletic activities are now female—up from a mere 7 percent in 1972. [20]
- Fifty-five percent of adults are now aware that a high-fat diet contributes to heart disease, up from 29 percent in 1983. [21]
- The average fat content of the U.S. diet has dropped from 42 percent of calories to 37 percent since the 1970s. [22]
- The number of people who admitted to drinking and driving dropped to 28 percent in 1988, down from 37 percent in 1985. [23]

LIFE-STYLE AND LONGEVITY

Life-style affects not only risk of disease and accidents, but the overall length of life, as several large research studies have shown. A study of nearly 7,000 persons completed in 1974 found

FIGURE 2.3
Walking's Effect on Longevity

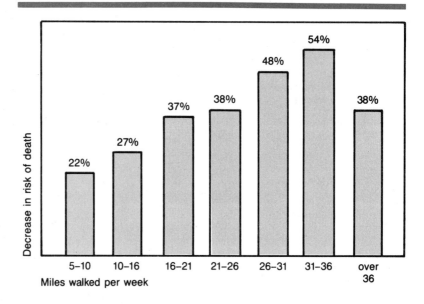

Source: Mark J. Tager and Jeffrey S. Harris, *Improving Your Odds: A Planning Guide for High-Level Health* (Beaverton, OR: Great Performance, Inc.), p. 5.

The study of Harvard alumni discussed in the text found that the more calories they expended on physical activity each week, the lower their risk of death. This chart shows how much your risk is lowered by various long-term walking regimens. Compared to a sedentary person, you may reduce your risk of death by 27%, for instance, if you walk 2 miles every day.

that men who practiced 7 particular life-style behaviors lived an average of 11 years longer than men who didn't. [24] For women, who already have a longer life expectancy than men, the increase in longevity was 7 years. The 7 practices found to be important were as follows:

* Not smoking
* Regular physical activity
* Moderate or no use of alcohol
* 7–8 hours of sleep regularly
* Maintaining a healthy weight
* Eating breakfast
* Eating 3 meals a day and not eating between meals [25]

FIGURE 2.4
The Health Benefits of Walking

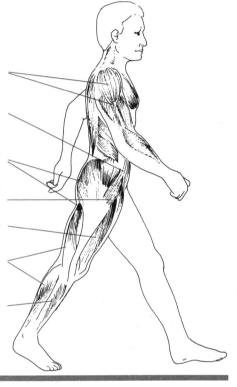

Arm and shoulder muscles: Swinging your arms while you walk exercises these muscles.

Abdominal muscles: Walking is an effective way to exercise these muscles, but requires proper posture to gain the most benefit.

Buttock and upper thigh muscles: Conditioned upper thigh muscles will help you counteract muscle fatigue, muscle soreness, and joint stiffness that sometimes result from exercise.

Hip flexor muscles: These muscles gain strength and flexibility as you lengthen your stride.

Quadriceps: Walking on an incline intensifies exercise for this muscle group.

Calf muscles and hamstrings: Walking on an incline intensifies exercise for this group. Stretching is particularly important to avoid injury to the achilles tendon and hamstrings.

Shin muscles: These muscles are exercised adequately with each simple walking step.

Walking regularly for exercise will strengthen the heart, shape and tone the muscles in the legs, hips, buttocks, and abdomen, and increase muscle mass and endurance.

A 45-year-old man who had only 3 or fewer of these habits could expect to live another 22 years, to the age of 67. But a 45-year-old man with 6 or 7 of these habits could expect to live another 33 years, to the age of 78. Not only length of life, but the quality of the years improved as well. Those men who practiced 6 or 7 of these behaviors were as healthy as men *30 years younger* who followed 2 or fewer practices. [26]

Regular exercise appears to be one of the most important factors contributing to a long, healthy life. Some of the best evidence yet that exercise increases longevity comes from a recent study conducted at the Institute for Aerobics Research in Dallas, Texas. [27] More than 13,000 people participated for an

(continued on p. 33)

Healthstyle: A Self Test

All of us want good health. But many of us do not know how to be as healthy as possible. Health experts now describe *lifestyle* as one of the most important factors affecting health. In fact, it is estimated that as many as seven of the ten leading causes of death could be reduced through common-sense changes in lifestyle. That's what this brief test, developed by the Public Health Service, is all about. Its purpose is simply to tell you how well you are doing to stay healthy. The behaviors covered in the test are recommended for most Americans. Some of them may not apply to persons with certain chronic diseases or handicaps, or to pregnant women. Such persons may require special instructions from their physicians.

Cigarette Smoking	Almost Always	Some-times	Almost Never
If you *never smoke,* enter a score of 10 for this section and go to the next section on *Alcohol and Drugs.*			
1. I avoid smoking cigarettes.	2	1	0
2. I smoke only low tar and nicotine cigarettes *or* I smoke a pipe or cigars.	2	1	0

Smoking Score: _____

Alcohol and Drugs	Almost Always	Some-times	Almost Never
1. I avoid drinking alcoholic beverages *or* I drink no more than 1 or 2 drinks a day.	4	1	0
2. I avoid using alcohol or other drugs (especially illegal drugs) as a way of handling stressful situations or the problems in my life.	2	1	0
3. I am careful not to drink alcohol when taking certain medicines (for example, medicine for sleeping, pain, colds, and allergies), or when pregnant.	2	1	0
4. I read and follow the label directions when using prescribed and over-the-counter drugs.	2	1	0

Alcohol and Drugs Score: _____

Eating Habits	Almost Always	Some-times	Almost Never
1. I eat a variety of foods each day, such as fruits and vegetables, whole grain breads and cereals, lean meats, dairy products, dry peas and beans, and nuts and seeds.	4	1	0
2. I limit the amount of fat, saturated fat, and cholesterol I eat (including fat on meats, eggs, butter, cream, shortenings, and organ meats such as liver).	2	1	0
3. I limit the amount of salt I eat by cooking with only small amounts, not adding salt at the table, and avoiding salty snacks.	2	1	0
4. I avoid eating too much sugar (especially frequent snacks of sticky candy or soft drinks).	2	1	0

Eating Habits Score: _____

Exercise/Fitness	Almost Always	Some-times	Almost Never
1. I maintain a desired weight, avoiding overweight and underweight.	3	1	0
2. I do vigorous exercises for 15–30 minutes at least 3 times a week (examples include running, swimming, brisk walking).	3	1	0
3. I do exercises that enhance my muscle tone for 15–30 minutes at least 3 times a week (examples include yoga and calisthenics).	2	1	0
4. I use part of my leisure time participating in individual, family, or team activities that increase my level of fitness (such as gardening, bowling, golf, and baseball).	2	1	0

Exercise/Fitness Score: _____

Stress Control	Almost Always	Some-times	Almost Never
1. I have a job or do other work that I enjoy.	2	1	0
2. I find it easy to relax and express my feelings freely.	2	1	0

	Almost Always	Some-times	Almost Never
3. I recognize early, and prepare for, events or situations likely to be stressful for me.	2	1	0
4. I have close friends, relatives, or others whom I can talk to about personal matters and call on for help when needed.	2	1	0
5. I participate in group activities (such as church and community organizations) or hobbies that I enjoy.	2	1	0

Stress Control Score: _____

Safety	Almost Always	Some-times	Almost Never
1. I wear a seat belt while riding in a car.	2	1	0
2. I avoid driving while under the influence of alcohol and other drugs.	2	1	0
3. I obey traffic rules and the speed limit when driving.	2	1	0
4. I am careful when using potentially harmful products or substances (such as household cleaners, poisons, and electrical devices).	2	1	0
5. I avoid smoking in bed.	2	1	0

Safety Score: _____

What Your Scores Mean to YOU

Scores of 9 and 10

Excellent! Your answers show that you are aware of the importance of this area to your health. More important, you are putting your knowledge to work for you by practicing good health habits. As long as you continue to do so, this area should not pose a serious health risk. It's likely that you are setting an example for your family and friends to follow. Since you got a very high test score on this part of the test, you may want to consider other areas where your scores indicate room for improvement.

Scores of 6 to 8

Your health practices in this area are good, but there is room for improvement. Look again at the items you answered with a "Sometimes" or "Al-

most Never." What changes can you make to improve your score? Even a small change can often help you achieve better health.

Scores of 3 to 5

Your health risks are showing! Would you like more information about the risks you are facing and about why it is important for you to change these behaviors? Perhaps you need help in deciding how to successfully make the changes you desire. In either case, help is available.

Scores of 0 to 2

Obviously, you were concerned enough about your health to take the test, but your answers show that you may be taking serious and unnecessary risks with your health. Perhaps you are not aware of the risks and what to do about them. You can easily get the information and help you need to improve, if you wish. The next step is up to you.

YOU Can Start Right Now!

In the test you just completed were numerous suggestions to help you reduce your risk of disease and premature death. Here are some of the most significant:

Avoid cigarettes. Cigarette smoking is the single most important preventable cause of illness and early death. It is especially risky for pregnant women and their unborn babies. Persons who stop smoking reduce their risk of getting heart disease and cancer. So if you're a cigarette smoker, think twice about lighting that next cigarette. If you choose to continue smoking, try decreasing the number of cigarettes you smoke and switching to a low tar and nicotine brand.

Follow sensible drinking habits. Alcohol produces changes in mood and behavior. Most people who drink are able to control their intake of alcohol and to avoid undesired, and often harmful, effects. Heavy, regular use of alcohol can lead to cirrhosis of the liver, a leading cause of death. Also, statistics clearly show that mixing drinking and driving is often the cause of fatal or crippling accidents. So if you drink, do it wisely and in moderation. ***Use care in taking drugs.*** Today's greater use of drugs—both legal and illegal—is one of our most serious health risks. Even some drugs prescribed by your doctor can be dangerous if taken when drinking alcohol or before driving. Excessive or continued use of tranquilizers (or "pep pills") can cause physical and mental problems. Using or experimenting with illicit drugs such as marijuana, heroin, cocaine, and PCP may lead to a number of damaging effects or even death.

Eat sensibly. Overweight individuals are at greater risk for diabetes, gall bladder disease, and high blood pressure. So it makes good sense to maintain proper weight. But good eating habits also mean holding down the amount of fat (especially saturated fat), cholesterol, sugar and salt in your diet. If you must snack, try nibbling on fresh fruits and vegetables. You'll feel better—and look better, too.

Exercise regularly. Almost everyone can benefit from exercise—and there's some form of exercise almost everyone can do. (If you have any doubt, check first with your doctor.) Usually, as little as 15–30 minutes of vigorous exercise three times a week will help you have a healthier heart, eliminate excess weight, tone up sagging muscles, and sleep better. Think how much difference all these improvements could make in the way you feel!

Learn to handle stress. Stress is a normal part of living; everyone faces it to some degree. The causes of stress can be good or bad, desirable or undesirable (such as a promotion on the job or the loss of a spouse). Properly handled, stress need not be a problem. But unhealthy responses to stress—such as driving too fast or erratically, drinking too much, or prolonged anger or grief—can cause a variety of physical and mental problems. Even on a very busy day, find a few minutes to slow down and relax. Talking over a problem with someone you trust can often help you find a satisfactory solution. Learn to distinguish between things that are "worth fighting about" and things that are less important.

Be safety conscious. Think "safety first" at home, at work, at school, at play, and on the highway. Buckle seat belts and obey traffic rules. Keep poisons and weapons out of the reach of children, and keep emergency numbers by your telephone. When the unexpected happens, you'll be prepared.

Where Do You Go From Here:

Start by asking yourself a few frank questions: *Am I really doing all I can to be as healthy as possible? What steps can I take to feel better? Am I willing to begin now?* If you scored low in one or more *sections* of the test, decide what changes you want to make for improvement. You might pick that aspect of your lifestyle where you feel you have the best chance for success and tackle that one first. Once you have improved your score there, go on to other areas.

If you already have tried to change your health habits (to stop smoking or exercise regularly, for example), don't be discouraged if you haven't yet succeeded. The difficulty you have encountered may be due to influences you've never really thought about—such as advertising—or to a lack of support and encouragement. Understanding these influences is an important step toward changing the way they affect you.

There's Help Available. In addition to personal actions you can take on your own, there are community programs and groups (such as the YMCA or the local chapter of the American Heart Association) that can assist you and your family to make the changes you want to make. If you want to know more about these groups or about health risks, contact your local health department or the National Health Information Clearinghouse. There's a lot you can do to stay healthy or to improve your health—and there are organizations that can help you. Start a new HEALTHSTYLE today!

Source: National Health Information Clearinghouse, Washington, DC.

average of 8 years. Compared to nonexercisers, the death rate over the 8 years was significantly lower among those who obtained the equivalent of a 30- to 60-minute brisk walk every day (60 percent lower for men and 48 percent lower for women).

A study of 17,000 Harvard alumni followed their exercise levels and **mortality rates** for 16 years. [28] The men who walked often or were otherwise physically active had considerably lower death rates during the years of the study. Walking only 2 miles a day reduced risk of death by 27 percent, and walking 5 miles a day reduced risk by 54 percent.

Positive life-style habits don't just help us live longer, they help us live better, too. Again, exercise is one of the most important factors. Physically active people report that as a result of exercise they feel more creative, have more energy, are more relaxed, and feel more self-assured. They also report less tension, anger, and **depression**. [29]

ASSESSING YOUR HEALTH RISKS

A lifetime of good health does not happen by accident—it takes a healthy environment and personal awareness, knowledge, and commitment. Most of us have some idea of the positive and negative aspects of our current health habits but are less sure which habits will hurt or help in the long run. Since time and motivation are common constraints, it helps to learn where it is most effective to place one's efforts. A good place to start is by filling out a questionnaire, such as the one above, that appraises your health risks in areas where research has shown definite connections between personal life-style behaviors and the likelihood of a long, healthy life. Based on your results, you can plan new priorities in your day-to-day behaviors. Ⓦ

Did You Know That . . .

There are several key factors that influence your overall health. They include weight, cigarette smoking, exercise, blood pressure, safe driving, alcohol consumption, and cholesterol level.

Mortality rate: The number of individual deaths occurring in a given population or group, usually expressed in relation to some baseline figure as in deaths per 100,000.

Depression: A mental state characterized by extreme sadness or dejection that persists for an extended period of time.

CHAPTER

3

The Life-Style Diseases

MOST DISEASES THAT KILL Americans prematurely today are not caused by foreign organisms, such as viruses and bacteria, and they are not sudden in onset – they are caused, slowly but surely, by the way we live. Our inactivity, fatty diets, smoking and drinking habits, and nonchalance about routine safety matters take their toll in early disabilities and deaths, which are unnecessary, tragic, and costly. The number of common diseases, illnesses, and injuries influenced by our daily life-style choices are many: heart disease, cancer, stroke, lung disease, diabetes, osteoporosis, motor vehicle and other accidents, and **cirrhosis of the liver**, among others. Most of these are on the "top 10" list of leading causes of death. But, as one observer puts it, "the American way of life need not be hazardous to your health." Simple changes that lead to feeling better in the short term and reducing the likelihood of disease in the long term are within easy reach.

CARDIOVASCULAR DISEASE

Cardiovascular disease, disease of the heart or its blood vessels, is the leading cause of death in industrialized countries, killing close to 1 million people annually in the United States alone. An additional 42 million have some form of cardiovascular disease, and 1.5 million Americans suffer nonfatal heart attacks each year (1,200 people each day). [1]

Coronary artery disease is the most common type of cardiovascular disease. Gradually and silently over the years, the arteries that supply blood to the heart become narrowed by deposits of fatty material in their walls. When an artery becomes

---

Cirrhosis (of the liver): A disease that causes scarring and decreased functioning of the liver. It can be caused by chronic liver inflammation, hepatitis B, or chronic alcoholism.

Cardiovascular disease: Any of several diseases of the heart and its blood vessels.

Coronary artery disease: Disease of the blood vessels near the heart in which the arteries become narrowed and clogged with raised patches known as atherosclerotic plaque. Atherosclerotic plaque consists of decaying muscle cells, fibrous tissue, clumps of blood platelets, cholesterol, lipoproteins, and sometimes calcium.

34

FIGURE 3.1
Atherosclerosis

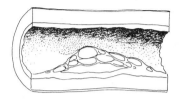
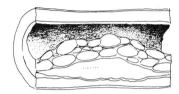

Normal arterial wall   Fat particles attach to artery   Partial blockage of artery
                           wall forming plaque

Atherosclerosis occurs when fatty substances such as cholesterol build up inside the coronary arteries. When the flow of blood to portions of the heart is restricted or blocked, a heart attack occurs.

clogged with debris to the point that blood cannot reach a portion of the heart muscle, a **heart attack** occurs, the result of the heart tissue being deprived of oxygen.

Men are over twice as likely to develop coronary artery disease as women, although the incidence in women has been steadily rising in recent years; it is the number-one killer of women as well as men. The likelihood of developing coronary artery disease also increases with age for both men and women. Once women reach **menopause**, changes in the production of sex hormones cause women's chances of suffering cardiovascular disease to catch up with those of men. Genetics plays a role, too; some families have a higher-than-average incidence of cardiovascular disease.

Although gender, age, and genetic makeup influence susceptibility to cardiovascular disease, they are obviously factors one cannot do much about. Other major risk factors are within control, however: smoking, high blood **cholesterol**, hypertension (high blood pressure), and lack of exercise. Other factors that increase risk are being overweight, having diabetes, drinking alcohol excessively, taking birth control pills, and having high levels of unmanaged stress. One eminent cardiologist feels the evidence is strong enough to say unequivocally, "Heart disease before [age] 80 is your own fault." [2]

Having one of these risk factors present increases risk, but having more than one factor present dramatically increases the likelihood of developing cardiovascular disease. For example,

Heart attack: The sudden death of part of the heart muscle. Also known as myocardial infarction.

Menopause: The cessation of menstruation in the female, typically between the ages of 45 and 50.

Cholesterol: A fat-like substance found in animal foods and also manufactured by the body. Cholesterol is essential to nerve and brain cell function and to the synthesis of sex hormones and is also a component of bile acids used to aid fat digestion. It is also a part of atherosclerotic plaques that accumulate on artery walls (see "Coronary artery disease").

FIGURE 3.2

Estimated Percentage of U.S. Population Having Selected Risk Factors for Coronary Heart Disease

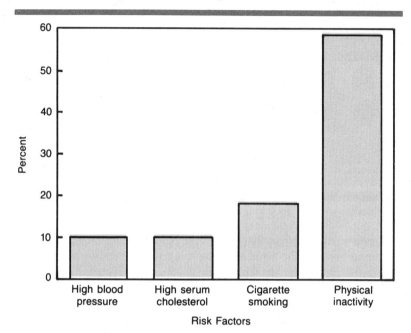

Source: "Protective Effect of Physical Activity on Coronary Heart Disease," *Mortality and Morbidity Weekly Report*, Vol. 36, No. 26, 10 July 1987, p. 429.

More Americans are at risk for heart disease because of physical inactivity than because of any other manageable risk factor.

smokers have 3 times the nonsmokers' risk of developing heart disease, but women who both smoke and take birth control pills are up to 39 times more likely to have a heart attack than women who do neither, according to the American Heart Association. [3] Even if a risk factor is present that cannot be changed, such as a genetic predisposition, research shows that the chance of develop- ing cardiovascular disease can be greatly reduced by taking charge of the manageable risk factors. Three of these factors deserve a closer look—smoking, blood cholesterol, and exercise.

Smoking
Smoking one pack of cigarettes a day triples the risk of death from cardiovascular disease. [4] A single cigarette reduces the

amount of blood the heart pumps with each beat, causing it to work far harder than necessary to pump blood through the 60,000 miles of blood vessels in the body.

Smoking damages the cardiovascular system by raising blood pressure and cholesterol, changing factors in the blood to cause increased clotting, constricting blood vessels, and speeding the heart rate. Smokers have elevated **carbon monoxide** levels and carry 20 percent less oxygen in their blood than nonsmokers, a factor that affects the functioning of all organs, not just the heart. On the other hand, once a smoker quits, the damaged cardiovascular system repairs itself within 5 to 10 years, and heart disease risk is cut in half. [5]

Cholesterol

Pathologists at the turn of the century noticed a common condition in the bodies of heart attack victims—their blood vessels were clogged with a yellowish substance, and arteries were hard and calcified. [6] The predominant ingredient in the yellowish substance? Cholesterol. Much research has gone on since then to clarify the role of this fat-like compound in heart disease.

Several major studies and numerous smaller ones have clearly shown that elevated blood cholesterol increases the risk of cardiovascular disease. A small percentage of the population has a genetic predisposition to develop high blood cholesterol. For the majority of the population, however, manageable life-style factors are the main cause of elevated blood cholesterol. The most prevalent are smoking, not exercising, and consuming a diet high in **saturated fats** and cholesterol. Of the two dietary factors, saturated fats are the biggest contributor—they raise blood cholesterol levels even more than the cholesterol in food does. These and other dietary factors are discussed in chapter 4.

The cholesterol picture is complicated by the fact that two major forms of cholesterol occur in the blood, **LDL cholesterol** and **HDL cholesterol**. LDL cholesterol is the "bad" kind, on its way to being deposited in the arteries. HDL cholesterol is the "good" kind, a scavenger compound carrying cholesterol out of the arteries. A low level of HDL cholesterol is thought by some cardiovascular researchers to be the most significant risk factor for disease because it indicates that the body is not able to clear cholesterol from the arteries adequately.

Harmful LDL cholesterol is raised by saturated fat and cholesterol in the diet. Beneficial HDL cholesterol is raised by exercise but lowered by smoking. To have an optimum ratio of "good" to "bad" forms of cholesterol, one needs to eat a diet low in

Carbon monoxide (CO): A colorless, odorless, and highly toxic gas formed as a by-product during the incomplete combustion of fossil fuels; it is also found in coal gas, the exhaust of internal combustion engines, and cigarette smoke.

Pathologist: A person who studies disease, particularly its causes, processes, and effects on the body.

Saturated fat: Organic acids containing carbon, oxygen, and the maximum quantity of hydrogen possible, combined with an oily alcohol called glycerol. Palm oil, coconut oil, and most animal fats are highly saturated.

LDL cholesterol: A form of cholesterol that is deposited in the walls of arteries, contributing to the process of atherosclerosis. It is increased by overconsumption of saturated fat and cholesterol and contributes to the risk of heart disease.

HDL cholesterol: A lipid compound containing cholesterol removed from the arteries; also termed the "good" form of cholesterol because high levels are desirable and reduce the risk of heart disease.

fat and cholesterol (to keep the "bad" LDL cholesterol low) *and* obtain regular exercise and forgo smoking (to keep the "good" HDL cholesterol high).

Vigorous exercise alone, although very important, may not protect one from heart disease, since a low-fat diet is equally important in order to keep LDL cholesterol low. The exerciser who says "I don't need to worry about what I eat, I burn it off" is hanging onto a potentially harmful misconception.

The process of **atherosclerosis**, the buildup of fatty deposits in arteries, begins as early as age 15. Healthy habits are thus as important in the teenage years, twenties, and thirties as they are during middle age and older years.

Exercise

"Did you brush your teeth today? Did you exercise? How long can you live without your teeth? How long can you live without your heart?" So begins a lecture by one fitness expert. The heart, the most important muscle in the body, is the muscle most ignored by people in industrialized nations.

Men who are sedentary have twice the risk of a heart attack as men who are moderately active and triple the rate of heart attack compared to men who are vigorous exercisers. In addition, when heart attacks do occur in nonexercisers, they are three times more likely to be fatal than when they occur in exercisers. [7]

Less than half the population in the United States is regularly active, and it is estimated only 10 percent of the population engages in the type of exercise that strengthens the heart muscle and prevents heart disease. [8]

The type of exercise that makes the heart more fit is termed **aerobic exercise**. Examples of aerobic exercise are brisk walking, jogging, swimming, cycling, and rowing. These activities share in common the ability to raise the heart rate to a necessary threshold zone and maintain it there for a sustained period of time (15 to 20 minutes or more). These activities also work the large muscle groups of the body. They are not "stop and go" activities, such as baseball, and they can be carried out at a level of intensity that does not cause huffing and puffing, as more vigorous sports do. The details of aerobic exercise are discussed further in chapter 4.

Aerobic activities condition the heart to pump more blood with each beat. Weight-lifting, calisthenics, and stretching do not have this effect. After a few weeks of regular aerobic exercise, the **resting heart rate** goes down (the heartbeats per minute while the body is at rest), one indication that the heart has become

Atherosclerosis: A form of hardening of the arteries in which a substance known as plaque gradually accumulates on artery walls, causing the blood vessels to lose elasticity and the arterial openings to narrow.

Aerobic exercise: A form of exercise that increases respiration, intake of oxygen, heart rate, and cardiovascular fitness.

Resting heart rate: The heart rate (beats per minute) while an individual is completely at rest, most accurately determined while still lying down following a night's sleep.

FIGURE 3.3
The Health Benefits of Exercise

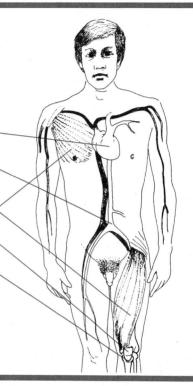

Heart: Aerobic exercise increases the size and stamina of the heart muscle, conditioning the heart to circulate a greater volume of blood with each beat, lowering the risk of heart disease and heart attack.

Circulation: Exercise increases the amount of oxygen in the bloodstream, and the level of HDL cholesterol in the blood. It lowers blood pressure, which helps prevent stroke and heart attack.

Muscles: Exercise increases the oxygen supply to muscles while strengthening and toning them, and increasing coordination.

Joints: Exercise keeps the joints supple and prevents joint disorders by thickening the cartilage.

Bones: Regular exercise thickens the bones and inhibits loss of calcium from the bones, preventing osteoporosis.

Besides tightening and toning muscles, aerobic exercise also strengthens the heart, stimulates the building of new blood vessels which promotes better circulation, and often reduces the level of fat in the blood.

stronger. The heart can now beat fewer times per minute to accomplish the job of pushing blood throughout the body. If, through exercise, one's heart rate decreases by 2 beats per minute (for example, from an initial resting rate of 72 beats per minute to 70 beats per minute), this amounts to 2,880 fewer beats each day, 20,160 fewer beats per week, and 1,048,320 less per year!

The wear and tear saved on the heart is considerable. Aerobic exercise also stimulates the building of new blood vessels, which promotes better circulation of blood and oxygen, providing alternative pathways to organs, especially the heart, should a blood vessel become clogged. Exercise also helps control blood cholesterol levels by raising the cholesterol-scavenging capabilities of the blood, the beneficial HDL cholesterol.

American Cancer Society's Guidelines to Reduce Risk for Cancer

1. Eat more cabbage family foods (broccoli, cauliflower, brussels sprouts, cabbage, kale).

2. Eat more high-fiber foods.

3. Choose fruits and vegetables with vitamin A (beta-carotene).

4. Choose foods with vitamin C.

5. Control body weight.

6. Trim fat from the diet.

7. Eat salt-cured, smoked, and nitrite-cured foods only occasionally or not at all.

8. Stop cigarette smoking.

9. Go easy on alcohol.

10. Avoid exposing your skin to too much sun and wear sunscreen.

Source: Adapted from *Taking Control: 10 Steps to a Healthier Life and Reduced Cancer Risk* (New York: American Cancer Society, 1985).

CANCER

Cancer is the second leading cause of death in the United States, responsible for approximately 22 percent of deaths. Cancer of the lung is the most frequent type (440,000 deaths yearly), followed closely by colon, breast, and prostate cancer.

As many as 75 percent of cancers are life-style–related—caused primarily by tobacco use, dietary fat, obesity, and alcohol. [9] The degree of known cancer risk because of food additives, industrial pollutants, pesticides, and other environmental factors, although of great concern, appears small in comparison to these major risk factors.

Tobacco
Not smoking is the single most effective step one can take to lower cancer risk. Lung cancer accounts for 15 to 25 percent of all

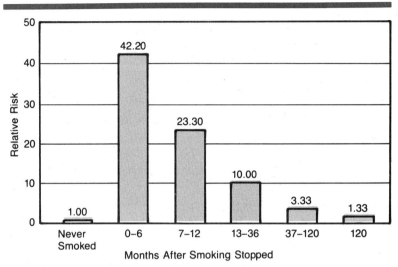

FIGURE 3.4
Risk of Lung Cancer After Smoking Cessation

Source: Donald Vickery, M.D., *Lifeplan* (Reston, VA: Vicktor, Inc., 1990), p. 151.

Quitting smoking eventually lowers lung cancer risk almost to that of a nonsmoker.

Did You Know That . . .

Alcohol seems to increase the cancer-causing effects of smoking. A person who smokes a pack of cigarettes and consumes 1 alcoholic drink per day is 4 times more likely to contract oral cancer than a total abstainer.

cancers, and smoking is clearly the most frequent cause. [10] Not breathing second-hand smoke is important, too. Research now shows that people exposed to the smoke of others have increased rates of lung cancer and respiratory infections. [11] The children of smokers with lung cancer, if they go on to become smokers themselves, have a 15 to 25 times higher likelihood of developing lung cancer than if they do not become smokers. [12] Smoking is also associated with cancers of the **esophagus**, stomach, and **pancreas**, especially in heavy drinkers.

Smokeless tobacco use (snuff and chewing tobacco) has increased among people under age 24, and although many harmful chemicals present in smoke are absent when this form of tobacco is used, risk of cancer of the mouth, stomach, and esophagus remains. The **nicotine** is still present, increasing heart disease risk. Addiction to tobacco occurs just as with smoking and, in fact, many smokeless tobacco users go on to become smokers.

Diet and Exercise

Excessive intake of any type of dietary fat, whether saturated or unsaturated, is associated with increased cancer risk, partic-

Esophagus: The tubular structure located immediately behind the windpipe (trachea) that connects the mouth and the stomach.

Pancreas: A long, tapered, irregularly shaped gland behind the stomach that secretes a variety of digestive enzymes and hormones including insulin, which regulates the level of glucose (sugar) in the blood.

Nicotine: A poisonous alkaloid that is the chief psychoactive ingredient of tobacco.

ularly of the breast and colon. Most Americans need to reduce fat intake by approximately 25 percent to meet current guidelines for a diet containing no more than 30 percent of calories from fat. In addition, the fiber found in whole wheat and other whole grains may be beneficial in preventing cancer of the colon.

Some research, most notably the study of 17,000 Harvard alumni who were followed for several years, indicates that regular exercise reduces deaths from cancer as well as from heart disease. [13]

Sun Worshipping

Too much time in the sun without adequate protection significantly adds to the threat of skin cancer. This disease is on the increase, in part because of the thinning of the earth's protective ozone layer, and in part because of the whims of fashion—the popularity of the dark tan. Incidence of malignant **melanoma**, a very deadly form of cancer, has risen alarmingly in recent years. At highest risk are those with fair skin and blonde or red hair, and those who freckle easily, live at high altitudes, or spend a lot of time outdoors.

Simple steps to take to prevent skin cancer are using sunblock, wearing hats, and limiting exposure to sun, especially during the middle of the day. In particular, sunburns should be avoided. Severe sunburns in children are associated with development of skin cancer later in life. Even without the skin being visibly burned, the more time one spends in the sun, the higher the risk.

CEREBROVASCULAR DISEASE

Melanoma: A skin cancer originating in the pigment-secreting cells of the skin that is highly malignant and may cause death.

Cerebrovascular disease: Injury to the brain through a thrombosis or clot in a blood vessel of the brain; also called a stroke.

Thrombosis: Coagulation of the blood into a clot that impedes circulation.

Hypertension: A chronic condition of high blood pressure, leading to increased risk for cardiovascular disease, stroke, and kidney disease.

Cerebrovascular disease, or stroke, is brain damage that occurs when blood vessels in the brain hemorrhage or when a blockage or blood clot called a **thrombosis** occurs. Control of hypertension (high blood pressure) over the last two decades has resulted in a remarkable decrease in occurrence of cerebrovascular disease. Since 1972, deaths due to stroke have dropped 48 percent. [14] It remains the third leading cause of death, however, and is largely preventable.

Factors that increase risk of stroke include **hypertension** (by far the most significant), overweight, diabetes, and birth control pills. In addition, the factors that increase risk of cardiovascular disease are major risk factors for stroke as well—a high-fat diet, smoking, and lack of exercise can result in clogged blood vessels in the brain as well as the heart.

FIGURE 3.5
Cumulative Decline in Age-Adjusted Stroke Death Rates

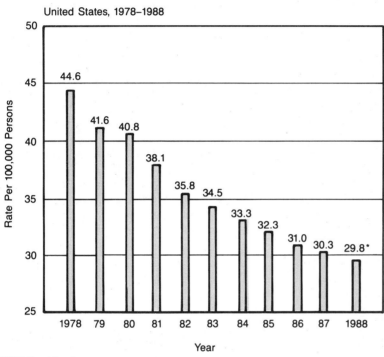

United States, 1978–1988

*1988 Provisional

Source: National Center for Health Statistics, Public Health Service, Department of Health and Human Services, and the American Heart Association.

Control of high blood pressure over the last two decades has resulted in a remarkable decrease in stroke death rates.

Hypertension

Only a small percentage of people with hypertension suffer strokes, but hypertension is the leading risk factor. Hypertension can occur as a result of other diseases, such as kidney disease, but it more commonly develops in the absence of disease. One-third to one-half of all cases of hypertension have developed in response to sodium intake, so limiting salt and other sources of **sodium** in the diet is important. [15] Other factors include the consumption of too much alcohol. Too little **calcium** (found primarily in milk and milk products) or too little potassium (found in fruits and vegeta-

Did You Know That . . .

Normal blood pressure for an adult is said to be 120/80 (systolic pressure/diastolic pressure) and is measured in millimeters of mercury.

Sodium: A mineral that helps regulate the body's water balance, maintain normal heart rhythm, and is vital to the transmission of impulses by the nervous system; the best known source of dietary sodium is sodium chloride (NaCl), table salt.

Calcium: A silvery, metallic element that is the most abundant mineral in the body; an adequate supply of the calcium is essential for the growth and maintenance of the skeletal system and to a broad range of bodily functions; the main dietary sources of calcium are dairy products, eggs, green vegetables, fruit, and fish.

bles) also appears to increase the likelihood of hypertension. [16] Exercise can effectively lower both blood pressure and stress levels. Unmanaged stress levels are thought to be a significant factor in high blood pressure, since release of stress hormones by the **adrenal glands** causes an increase in blood pressure.

OSTEOPOROSIS

A total of 15 million people (25 percent of women over the age of 65 and nearly 13 percent of men over the age of 65) have **osteoporosis**, a painful condition in which bones become thin and porous with age. Of the 200,000 hip fractures in the United States each year, 160,000 are due to osteoporosis. All too often, a bone fracture in an older person leads to infection, poor healing, lengthy hospital stays, and a downward spiral in health. An estimated 32,000 deaths occur each year from the complications that follow a hip fracture in older adults. [17]

We tend to think that becoming shorter and bent over is an inevitable part of aging, but this is not so. Bone health in the later years depends considerably on life-style habits throughout life. Although bones stop growing in length in the late teens or early twenties, growth in bone density or hardness continues through the mid-30s. Minerals move in and out of bones on a daily basis, making the replacement through diet of the lost minerals important throughout life.

Exercise is a crucial factor in bone health. The bones in the right arm of a right-handed tennis player may be 15 percent denser than those in the left arm. Bones steadily lose calcium when one is inactive. Much calcium is lost from bones during just a few days of bed rest in the hospital, for example. Years ago, Gemini astronauts returning from orbit were found to have lost considerable amounts of calcium from their bones while in a zero-gravity environment. Astronauts now perform special exercises to put pressure on bones while in flight.

Several alcoholic drinks a day, smoking, eating too much protein, and consuming too much phosphorus (found in soft drinks, processed foods, and protein-rich animal foods) are factors that increase risk by causing a greater loss of calcium from bones.

Developing strong, dense bones before the age of 35 is thought to be the most important way to prevent osteoporosis. A diet providing calcium from low-fat milk products or other sources and regular, weight-bearing exercise result in healthy bones with large amounts of minerals in them. Vitamin D,

Adrenal glands: A small, triangular shaped pair of glands located on top of the kidneys that secrete hormones including adrenaline (epinephrine) directly into the bloodstream.

Osteoporosis: Increased porosity of the bones, leading to weakness and a greater likelihood of fractures.

FIGURE 3.6
Osteoporosis and Spinal Deformity

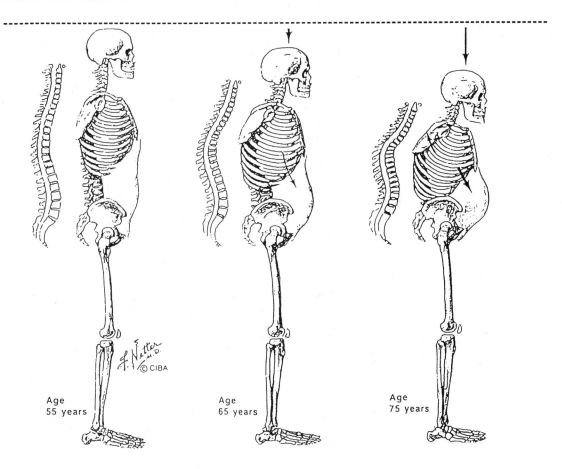

Age
55 years

Age
65 years

Age
75 years

Source: F. Kaplan, "Osteoporosis," *Clinical Symposia/CIBA,* Vol. 35, No. 5 (1983).

More frequent among women than men, osteoporosis is characterized by a continuing loss of bone mass. It can produce severe spinal deformity as shown here.

obtained from sunlight or through food, is also required for calcium use in the body. Research indicates that adults over age 50 may not get enough vitamin D. [18] At least fifteen minutes outdoors each day and consumption of vitamin D-fortified milk are ways to obtain this nutrient. Adequate calcium and vitamin

Table 3.1 Calcium in Foods

Food	Amount	Milligrams of Calcium
whole milk	1 cup	290
skim milk	1 cup	302
yogurt	1 cup	270
cheddar cheese	1 ounce	213
cottage cheese	$1/2$ cup	100
ice cream	1 cup	194
canned salmon	3.5 ounces	225
sardines	3 ounces	375
tofu	2 in. × 1 in. piece	154
spinach, cooked	$1/2$ cup	116
broccoli, cooked	$1/2$ cup	68
okra, cooked	$1/2$ cup	147
lentils	$1/2$ cup	25
lima beans	$1/2$ cup	40
orange	1	70
cornbread	2 in. square	133
blackstrap molasses	1 tbs.	137
raisins	3 tbs.	54

Recommended daily allowance for males and females age 15–24: 1200 mg, age 25 and older: 800 mg

Source: U.S. Department of Agriculture, Handbook No. 456.

The best way to avoid osteoporosis is to eat foods rich in calcium on a regular basis.

D intake and regular exercise remain important *after* age 35 as well. Swimming, though beneficial for the heart, by itself does not place enough pressure on bones to maintain their health, but a 30-minute daily walk, jog, or other weight-bearing activity will contribute significantly to bone health.

OVERWEIGHT

Being overweight is not uncommon in our sedentary society. As many as 20 to 30 percent of adults are 10 percent or more above their recommended weight. Overweight is a concern primarily because it increases the likelihood of developing several common diseases, including heart disease, cancer, hypertension, and diabetes. Having excess weight puts extra strain on joints, can aggravate arthritis, and can make any necessary surgery more difficult and risky. Being overweight also leads to lethargy and low self-esteem, conditions that affect how one feels day in and day out.

The causes of **obesity** (excess body fat) are complex and for some people may involve differences in fat cells, genetics, metabolic factors, and brain regulatory functions. But for most, the cause is far simpler: a sedentary life-style and a diet too high in concentrated calories from fat, sugar, or alcohol.

STRESS

Stress is an aspect of life difficult to measure and research, but one that appears to affect our health as much as diet, exercise, or cigarettes. Events that have the potential to cause stress are unavoidable. How strongly we react to the events determines the impact on our cardiovascular, nervous, and immune systems. When a situation is perceived as stressful, changes occur in hormones, nerves, blood pressure, breathing, and muscles. Either chronic low-level stress or a sudden, major stress can be a factor in hypertension, depression, **anxiety**, heart disease, some cancers, and lowered resistance to colds and infections. [19] Some experts estimate that as many as 85 percent of illnesses are stress-related and that the degree of absenteeism in work sites is a reflection of stress more than any other factor. [20]

Anything that brings change can cause stress–whether it is a negative event or a positive one. Being late for work, having a flat tire, losing a loved one, or having financial difficulties can produce stress. Similarly, being promoted to a new job, getting married, or retiring can be stressful events.

Many early warning signals of stress can occur, including headaches, muscle tension, allergies, nervous tics, anxiety, fatigue, and frequent colds. If stress is not coped with when these early signs appear, possible results include ulcers, high blood pressure, depression and other mental health problems, and an increased likelihood of major disease.

INJURIES

Accidents kill more young people than any other cause, accounting for 50 percent of fatalities that occur between the ages of 15

Obesity: The excessive accumulation of fat in the body to a level that, depending on the age, frame size, and height of the affected person, is considered undesirable.

Stress: Any external stimulus, whether physical or psychological, that necessitates resistance, change, or adaptation by the individual.

Anxiety: An emotional state characterized by uneasiness, apprehension, or fear.

FIGURE 3.7
Seat Belt Use

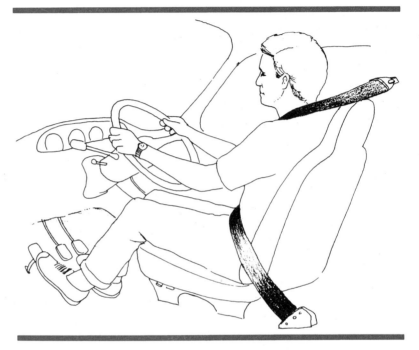

It is estimated that seat belt use can prevent 50 percent of all deaths resulting from motor vehicle accidents.

and 24. By age 44, accidents drop into fourth place as a cause of death. Motor vehicle accidents are by far the leading culprit, killing more than 140,000 Americans each year. Drownings, poisonings, and falls together account for 33 percent of fatal accidents, less than two-thirds as many deaths as motor vehicle accidents.

About two-thirds of states have mandatory seat belt laws. The resulting decrease in fatalities is as much as 33 percent. [21] All 50 states now require that infants and young children be in child safety restraints while in vehicles. Individuals who choose not to wear seat belts are far more likely to die in a crash than those who wear them—it is estimated that seat belt use can prevent 50 percent of motor vehicle deaths.

Fifteen percent of accidental deaths occur on the job (approximately 14,000 deaths each year). An additional 2.5 million disabling injuries occur in work sites yearly. Among those age 75 and older, falls are the most frequent type of accident. The death rate from injuries in older adults is more than $2^1/_2$ times that of teenagers and young adults. Deaths because of injury are really only the tip of the iceberg—an estimated 75 million serious or disabling injuries occur each year. [22]

Perhaps the word "accident" is a misnomer because it implies an occurrence of freak chance or something unavoidable. The

The Murder of Grabwell Grommet

On the morning of his 42nd birthday, Grabwell Grommet awoke to a peal of particularly ominous thunder. Glancing out the window with bleary eyes, he saw written in fiery letters across the sky:

"Someone is Trying To Kill You, Grabwell Grommet!"

With shaking hands, Grommet lit his first cigarette of the day. He didn't question the message. You don't question messages like that. His only question was, "Who?"

At breakfast as he salted his fried egg, he told his wife, Gratia, "Someone's trying to kill me."

"Who?" she asked with horror.

Grommet slowly stirred the cream and sugar into his coffee and shook his head. "I don't know," he said.

Convinced though he was, Grommet wasn't going to the police with his story. He decided his only course was to go about his daily routine and hope somehow to outwit his would-be murderer.

He tried to think on the drive to the office. But the frustration of making time by beating lights and switching lanes occupied him wholly. Nor, once behind his desk, could he find a moment, what with jangling phones, urgent memos and the problems and decisions piling up as they did each day.

It wasn't until his second martini at lunch that the full terror of his position struck him. It was all he could do to finish his lasagna.

"I can't panic," he said to himself, lighting his cigar. "I simply must live my life as usual."

So he worked till seven as usual. Drove home fast as usual. Ate a hearty dinner as usual. Had his two cocktails as usual. Studied business reports as usual. And he took his usual two Seconal capsules in order to get his usual six hours of sleep.

As the days passed, the man fully stuck to his routine. And as the months went by, he began to take a perverse pleasure in his ability to survive.

"Whoever's trying to get me," he'd say proudly to his wife, "hasn't got me yet. I'm too smart for him."

"Oh, please be careful," she'd reply, ladling him a second helping of beef stroganoff.

> The pride grew as he managed to go on living for years. But, as it must to all men, death came at last to Grabwell Grommet. It came at his desk on a particularly busy day. He was 53.
>
> His grief-stricken widow demanded a full autopsy.
>
> But it showed only emphysema, arteriosclerosis, duodenal ulcers, cirrhosis of the liver, cardiac necrosis, a cerebrovascular aneurism, pulmonary edema, obesity, circulatory insufficiency and a touch of lung cancer.
>
> "How glad Grabwell would have been to know," said the widow smiling proudly through her tears, "that he died of natural causes."
>
> Source: Arthur Hoppe

most important factor in accidents, however, is something over which one does have control—alcohol use. Alcohol is involved in over half of motor vehicle injuries and close to half of motorcycle injuries. Alcohol is a major factor in injuries to pedestrians, drownings, and job injuries as well.

Although wellness and personal health promotion often center upon changing fitness, nutrition, and other life-style habits, accidental injury remains a common threat to health and one fairly easy to control. Simple steps for preventing injuries are discussed in the next chapter.

THE CHOICE IS YOURS

Staying fit and healthy gives us the means to enjoy each day and be able to pursue and accomplish our goals over the course of a lifetime. In the next chapter, you will see that the life-style patterns that improve energy and well-being and that prevent major diseases are one and the same—and, the daily choices one needs to make, relatively simple and rewarding. W

Healthy Life-Style

BEING HEALTHY AND FIT in our society often requires swimming against the current and making some effort to implement positive changes in a gradual and enjoyable fashion. If one chooses simply to "go with the flow" of typical life-style habits, one is likely to wind up overweight, stressed, tired, and eventually suffering from one of the common chronic life-style diseases. On the other hand, by taking charge of just a few areas of one's life, well-being can be improved significantly. These important areas are fitness, **nutrition**, stress, smoking, alcohol and drug abuse, safety, and mental well-being.

THE FITNESS HABIT

Throughout history, humans have been active creatures out of necessity. It is only in recent times that the majority of people living in industrialized countries have become so sedentary. Rather than chop and carry firewood or shovel coal, we turn a dial or push a button for heat. Instead of walking to work and the neighborhood market, we drive. Mechanization of workplace tasks, power tools, kitchen mixers and food processors, motorized bikes, boats, and other recreational vehicles are examples of changes that have reduced the effort our bodies put forth. Over the course of a year, the difference can add up. The decrease in calories burned when a secretary switches from a manual typewriter to an electric typewriter for a year is the equivalent of 10 pounds of body fat! Although machines and technology allow us to accomplish more work with less effort, health suffers if the

Nutrition: The process by which we obtain the essential nutrients our bodies need to function.

51

resulting decrease in activity is not made up for somewhere else during the day.

Bodies, it seems, are made to be moved. Without exercise, muscle tone diminishes, **metabolism** slows, circulation and heart efficiency decrease, and bones lose strength. Conversely, regular exercise tones muscles and improves their strength and endurance, makes the heart stronger, improves circulation, improves physical appearance, burns body fat, raises metabolism, allows more oxygen to reach tissues, keeps bones strong, and helps lower blood cholesterol and blood pressure. Because of these physiological changes, exercise helps to reduce the risk of heart disease, cerebrovascular disease, osteoporosis, diabetes, overweight, and cancer. Research also indicates that exercisers are sick less often than sedentary people. [1]

Exercise is one of the most effective ways to promote relaxation and modify the body's response to stress. Numerous stress-related ailments, including headache, backache, sleep problems, ulcers, anxiety, fatigue, and depression, can be alleviated through regular activity. Exercisers also report changes in mental well-being—an increase in energy, self-esteem, relaxation, confidence, and alertness, as well as the fun and enjoyment of the activity itself.

Components of Fitness

Different types of fitness activities bring different benefits. Three major categories of fitness are flexibility, muscle strength and endurance, and aerobic or cardiovascular fitness.

Stretching improves flexibility and promotes back health, resilient muscles, injury prevention, and relaxation. Muscle-strengthening and muscular endurance activities include lifting weights, using weight resistance equipment, and performing calisthenics (such as abdominal exercises and push-ups). These improve muscle tone, appearance, and back health and afford the strength necessary to carry out the tasks of daily living, especially as a person ages. Aerobic exercise works the most important muscle, the heart, stimulating it to become stronger and circulate more oxygen. Other organs and muscles are trained to take in and use more oxygen as well, and the circulatory system becomes more efficient. In addition, aerobic activity burns fat, making it an essential aid for weight management and fat loss. Stretching, working out with weights, and calisthenics do not provide this same fat-burning benefit.

A well-rounded fitness program includes attention to all three areas: flexibility, muscular strength and endurance, and

Metabolism: The chemical and physical processes inside living cells comprising the building up of new and the breaking down of old substances and tissues. Energy is released in the process.

A lot of people put off exercising because they believe they don't have the time. They think that commuting to work mornings and evenings prevents them from exercising then, and that the days are too full of work. But all it takes is a little imagination. Exercise doesn't always mean jogging, doing sit-ups, or lifting weights in a health club. There are many strategies for fitting exercise into even the busiest schedule.

The Fast Track to Fitness

Brisk walking, for example, is good exercise. So instead of parking your car near the office or the train station, park a mile or two away and walk briskly to your destination. It will probably take you only an extra 15 to 20 minutes, and you'll be getting a moderately good aerobic workout.

Avoid elevators and escalators. Walking up several flights of stairs every day is superb exercise, considering the fact that your legs are lifting the total weight of your body at every step. If you work or live on a high floor of a building, get off the elevator a few floors below and walk up the last flights.

Getting into shape aerobically requires just three 20- to 30-minute sessions of vigorous activity per week. You don't have to jog 10 miles at a time or swim laps for an hour straight. So devoting about half your lunch break three times a week to fitness will get you on the fast track to health.

Source: *University of California Berkeley Wellness Letter,* Vol. 2, No. 3, December 1985, pp. 1–2.

Did You Know That . . .

The average American walks an estimated 115,000 miles during his or her lifetime.

aerobic fitness. It is aerobic exercise, however, that clearly yields the greatest health benefits, including increased mental well-being, longevity, lowered risk of heart disease and perhaps cancer, stronger bones, and control of body fat, diabetes, stress, and blood pressure. Aerobic exercise is simple to carry out – as simple as taking a brisk walk several times a week.

Aerobic Fitness To be beneficial, aerobic exercise must be vigorous enough to increase the breathing rate (aerobic means "using oxygen"), raise the heart rate for at least 15 to 20 minutes continuously, involve the use of large muscle groups, and be done at least 3 times a week.

Examples of activities that can accomplish this include brisk walking or hiking, light jogging, running, cycling, swimming, cross-country skiing, rowing, and aerobic dance. During these activities, the heart rate can be raised from its resting level to a **training zone**, in which it beats at a rate of 60 to 85 percent of its

Training zone: A range of heart rates (beats per minute) that effectively promotes cardiovascular fitness during exercise, generally defined as between 60 and 85 percent of an individual's maximum heart rate.

To make sure you are exercising at the speed and intensity that will increase cardiovascular fitness and burn body fat, monitor your heart rate.

Your target heart rate is determined by the following formula: 220 minus your age times 65–85% (this gives you a range of heart rates at which to exercise; choose whichever level is comfortable for you).

Your Fitness Target Zone

Count your pulse 5 minutes into your activity, once or twice in the middle, and at the end. If you are below your target zone, speed up or swing your arms as you walk to raise your heart rate. If you are above your target zone, slow down a bit. If your heart rate is within your target zone, you are exercising at a good aerobic level. (When cooling down afterward, keep moving slowly until your pulse is below 100.)

To determine your heart rate while exercising, count your pulse for only 10 seconds, multiply the number by 6, and compare it to the target zone you determined with the formula above. Or memorize your numbers on the following chart:

Age	Target Zone (10-second count)
19–21	22–27
22–30	21–26
31–39	20–25
40–48	19–23
49–57	18–23
58–66	17–21

maximum capability. Activity at this heart rate generally feels invigorating but not overly strenuous or exhausting.

When one works out at higher levels of intensity than this (as in sprinting and racquetball, for example), the fitness-producing aerobic training zone is exceeded, and one becomes increasingly anaerobic (without air), as evidenced by feeling out of breath and huffing and puffing. Although such high-intensity exercise can be useful for athletic training, it is not necessary for obtaining health benefits and in fact does not produce the same beneficial effects as less intense aerobic exercise. In addition, high-intensity exercise is more often associated with injuries, muscle and joint soreness, and overall discomfort or lack of enjoyment of the activity. High-intensity activity should be pursued if it is enjoyed,

(continued on p. 56)

FIGURE 4.1
Turn-of-the-Century Exercise Equipment

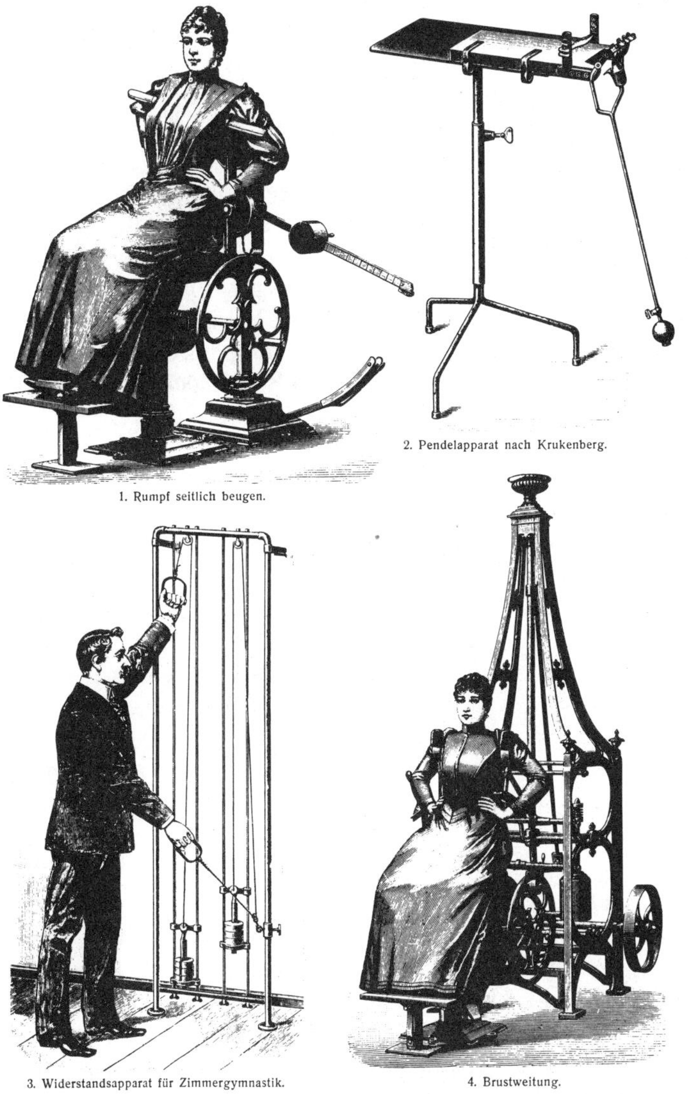
1. Rumpf seitlich beugen.
2. Pendelapparat nach Krukenberg.
3. Widerstandsapparat für Zimmergymnastik.
4. Brustweitung.

Source: Culver Pictures.

As illustrated in this German drawing from 1905, exercise equipment has been around longer than many people realize. Any health benefits obtained from using such equipment while wearing the restrictive clothing shown here are likely to have been limited.

Did You Know That . . .

The bicycle, a tool of aerobic exercise for many people today, was first invented by Karl D. von Sauerbronn in Germany in 1816.

but the misconception of "no pain, no gain" is just that—a misconception. Gentler forms of activity will produce substantial fitness benefits.

Muscle strengthening activities (such as weight lifting) and muscular endurance activities (such as sit-ups) can also raise the heart rate to the training zone, but little aerobic benefit is achieved because such activities have a different effect on the **circulatory system**. It is another common misconception that because such activities raise the heart rate and cause increased breathing, they are building aerobic fitness. With one exception, this is not the case. Some gyms and spas have "supercircuit" training equipment, a series of machines with pulleys and weights that work different muscle groups. By doing many repetitions with light weights and jogging in place between weight stations to keep the heart rate up, some aerobic benefit is achieved, although it is small in comparison to true aerobic activities. The American College of Sports Medicine, in its most recent exercise guidelines, states that such activity is not adequate for producing aerobic fitness. [2]

Stop-and-go activities, such as baseball and golf, are also not effective for aerobic conditioning because the heart is beating too slowly or the minimum 15-minute continuous time period is not maintained.

Research shows that in only 45 minutes a week—three 15-minute activity periods—significant improvements in health can be accomplished for the previously sedentary person. More activity than this provides additional benefits. Large studies have shown the most health benefits accrue when people engage in enough activity to burn 2,000 to 3,000 calories weekly. This is the equivalent of walking for 5 hours or jogging for 3 hours during the week. [3]

Put Activity in the Day

No increase in activity, however small, is without some benefit. A study of double-decker bus conductors in Great Britain, for example, showed they had fewer heart diseases than the bus drivers. Similarly, mail carriers with walking routes have fewer cases of heart disease than postal workers with desk jobs. [4] Taking the stairs instead of the elevator, parking the car farther from one's destination, staying out on the dance floor Saturday night, and participating in sports, gardening, yard work, hiking, and other outdoor activities can all add to fitness.

The pleasure that comes from being active, whether it is the peace of a solitary walk or the comraderie and fun of team sports,

Circulatory system: The system consisting of the heart and blood vessels which maintains the flow of blood throughout the body.

Starting an exercise habit is easy—maintaining it is more difficult. Remember, fitness activities come in all shapes and sizes, and variety is the spice of life. Try these ideas to stay motivated:

Ease into it
Do it with a friend
Try a new walking/jogging route

Keeping Exercise Fun

Enter a "Fun Run"
Buy a new pair of shoes
Take a weekend bike ride
Keep a fitness log
Sign up for a class

Exercise with a video
Start a lunchtime walking group at work
Take up gardening
Hit a tennis ball around with a friend
Bad weather? Try an indoor swimming pool or mall walking
Learn a new sport
Take dance classes
Good weather? Try an outdoor swimming pool
Buy a new pair of shorts
Walk the dog
Read a new book about your sport or activity
Have your fitness level tested
Spend time with other exercisers
Reward yourself periodically for staying active: dinner out, a movie, a
    new book, a massage
Subscribe to a health and fitness magazine
Lapsed into inactivity for a few weeks? Put on your shoes and take a
    walk at sunset
Join a sports team or club
Help a friend to start exercising
Go dancing! Keep moving!

Did You Know That . . .

Over 70 million Americans exercise regularly.

can add quality to life no matter what one's age or physical prowess. In fact, it appears it is never too late to become physically active and enjoy the rewards. People over age 64 are able to improve their cardiovascular fitness, flexibility, and muscle strength after only 4 months of regular exercise, even in the presence of high blood pressure, heart disease, lung disease, diabetes, and arthritis. [5] The oldest runner in the 26-mile 1990 New York marathon was 90 years old!

Including some enjoyable, aerobic activity in one's schedule 3 or more days each week is an irreplaceable part of a healthy life-style. (For additional information on fitness, see the book in this series entitled *Wellness: Exercise & Physical Fitness*.) [6]

EATING WELL

Although the typical American diet has many positive aspects, it is also composed of 37 percent fat and 18 percent sugar, contains a lot of sodium, a lot of cholesterol, not much **complex carbohydrate** (starch) or **fiber**, and, for some, too much alcohol. [7]

Why are these habits a problem? Too much fat of any type is associated with a higher likelihood of developing cancer. Too much saturated fat and cholesterol can clog arteries and increase the risk for heart disease. Too much sodium contributes to hypertension in some people. Too little fiber adds to the risk of gastrointestinal problems and colon cancer. Eating too few complex carbohydrate foods, which are low in fat and calories, means the diet is probably full of foods high in fat or sugar instead. Too much alcohol adds to the risk for cancer and cirrhosis of the liver, crowds nutritious foods from the diet by adding "empty" calories, and increases the risk for numerous illnesses.

Seven of the 10 leading causes of death are related to how we eat. During the last 20 years, several national health agencies have urged changes in the American way of eating, including the National Research Council of the National Academy of Sciences, the American Heart Association, the National Cancer Institute, the American Cancer Society, and the U.S. Department of Agriculture and Department of Health and Human Services. Canada and the European countries have made recommendations for their people very similar to the changes recommended for Americans. In the United States, recently released dietary guidelines include the following: [8]

Complex carbohydrate: A polysaccharide, or compound consisting of many sugar molecules linked together. Complex carbohydrates in the diet include starches and the fiber cellulose.

Fiber: Nondigestible residues of plant foods, primarily types of carbohydrates, some of which play a role in preserving the health of the gastrointestinal tract and lowering blood cholesterol.

- Reduce fat intake to no more than 30 percent of calories and reduce cholesterol to no more than 300 mg daily. For most Americans, this involves cutting about one-fourth of their current fat intake from the diet.
- Eat protein foods in moderation (4 to 6 ounces of meat, poultry, or fish daily are adequate). Many Americans consume $1^{1}/_{2}$ to 3 times more protein than they need.
- Eat more grains and legumes for complex carbohydrate and fiber (at least 6 servings daily). Many Americans need to double

(continued on p. 60)

Alcohol Poses Many Health Risks, Few Benefits

In the 1920's alcohol was considered evil and illegal. Today's concerns about alcohol focus on its health effects. While some studies show it may help prevent heart disease, others have linked it to breast cancer, high blood pressure and birth defects. Are there medical reasons to imbibe or to avoid alcohol completely?

Alcohol and Blood Pressure. Excessive alcohol intake may be the most common cause of secondary hypertension (high blood pressure for which the cause is known). U.S. population studies show 3 to 10 percent of high blood pressure in men is due to alcohol; in women, the percentage is lower. One obvious reason for the lower incidence of alcohol-induced hypertension in women is that fewer women drink. A more important reason may be that women react differently to alcohol.

Whereas the relationship between alcohol intake and blood pressure in men is linear—the more alcohol consumed, the higher the blood pressure—the relationship in women is U-shaped. That is, women who drink moderately (up to 20 grams of alcohol a day—the equivalent of about 8 ounces of wine) tend to have lower blood pressures than abstainers (1), while those who drink more have more hypertension.

In general, hypertension is 1.6 to 2.4 times more prevalent in heavy drinkers than in non-drinkers (1). But heavy drinking is defined in various ways in various studies, making study comparisons difficult. According to Michael J. Klag, M.D., M.P.H., Assistant Professor in the Department of Epidemiology at the Johns Hopkins Medical Institutions, at a level above three drinks a day, most people will experience a rise in blood pressure—4 to 6 points systolically (the top number in a blood pressure reading) and 2 to 3 points diastolically (the bottom number). Although these numbers may seem small, Dr. Klag stresses they are averages. "Some people will see less of an effect; others will experience higher blood pressures."

Alcohol and Heart Disease. Not all the news about alcohol is bad. Some studies suggest moderate drinking reduces people's risk of incurring the nation's #1 killer, heart disease. While previous studies have focused almost exclusively on men, a recent study has confirmed that alcohol reduces women's risk, too. The Nurse's Health Study of 87,000 women found that those drinking three to nine drinks a week had a 40 percent lower risk of heart disease compared to non-drinkers. (2) The study also found moderate drinkers to have a 30 percent lower risk of ischemic strokes (strokes due to blockage of blood vessels in the brain).

Researchers believe that alcohol may exert its protective effect by increasing levels of high density lipoproteins in the blood—the "good" cholesterol that helps protect against heart disease. It may also decrease slightly the blood's tendency to clot, thereby producing a protective effect against strokes caused by blood clots.

According to the Nurse's Health Study, however, drinking increases a woman's risk of a less common form of stroke. Hemorrhagic stroke (stroke from bleeding) was found to be two to three times more common in women who drank moderately.

In men, alcohol's effect on stroke risk is unclear, primarily because it hasn't been studied extensively. One study of men, the Honolulu Heart Program, showed that male drinkers, like women, experienced a two to three times greater risk of hemorrhagic stroke, but found no evidence of alcohol protecting them against ischemic stroke. (3)

Alcohol and Breast Cancer. One of the most highly publicized detrimental effects of alcohol also came from the Nurse's Health Study. It found that drinkers experienced a 30 percent increase in the risk for breast cancer. But according to Clark Heath, Vice President of Epidemiology and Statistics at the American Cancer Society, this is just one in a series of studies that disagree about alcohol's impact on breast cancer. "The data aren't so strong that you should worry if you have one drink a day," says Mr. Clark.

Meir Stampfer, M.D. Associate Physician at the Brigham and Women's Hospital in Boston and one of the principal investigators in the Nurse's Health Study, adds further perspective to the conflict: "Heart disease kills far more women than breast cancer. On the other hand, we don't know how to prevent breast cancer, while there are lots of ways to prevent heart disease."

Fetal Alcohol Syndrome. When it comes to drinking during pregnancy, experts generally agree there's no such thing as a safe amount of alcohol for women. Fetal alcohol syndrome (FAS) is among the three leading known causes of birth defects resulting in mental retardation. And it is the only preventable one among them.

Full blown fetal alcohol syndrome, with its accompanying physical and mental abnormalities, has been reported in infants of women who consumed as few as two drinks a day, according to Agnes Huber, Ph.D., R.D. immediate past president of the Nutrition and Dietetics Division of the American Association of Mental Retardation.

Alcohol negatively affects the developing fetus in two ways: It collapses blood vessels, depriving the fetus of oxygen and glucose, and it dries out cells, destroying neurons and damaging the developing brain.

What about the woman who drinks in the early weeks of pregnancy, before she is aware she's expecting? The best advice, according to Dr.

Huber, is to stop drinking as soon as she knows she is pregnant. Not every fetus whose mother drinks will have FAS. In fact, most infants of women who drink will not develop FAS. But because experts can't identify those who will, they recommend that women not drink at all during pregnancy.

Although alcohol has long been and is still promoted as an aid to breastfeeding, Dr. Huber advises against it. Alcohol is secreted in the breast milk and brain cells continue to be formed until a child is about two years of age.

To Drink or Not. Conflicting studies are the rule rather than the exception in alcohol research, primarily because of differences in the definition of what constitutes a drink, the number of drinks that make a person a "heavy drinker" and how accurate a person's recall is of his previous drinking.

Despite the conflicting findings, most experts agree that any possible health benefits from alcohol are small, and some feel its negative effects far outweigh any positive ones. The general consensus, then is that drinking's health benefits are neither cause to start drinking, nor should they be used as an excuse to continue doing so.

—Marsha Hudnall, M.S., R.D.

(1) *Postgraduate Medicine*, pp. 273–274, June, 1984.
(2) *The New England Journal of Medicine*, pp. 273–276, August 4, 1988.
(3) *Journal of the American Medical Association*, pp. 2311–2314, May 2, 1986.

Source: *Environmental Nutrition*, Vol. 12, No. 7, July 1989, pp. 1, 6.

their intake of complex carbohydrate foods to meet this guideline.
- Consume 5 servings daily of fruits and vegetables. These provide fiber and vitamins A and C, which reduce cancer risk, and potassium, which may reduce the risk of hypertension.
- Limit sodium intake to 6 grams daily (the equivalent of 1 teaspoon of salt). The average sodium intake for Americans is the equivalent of 2 to 4 teaspoons of salt per day.

FIGURE 4.2
Eating Healthy

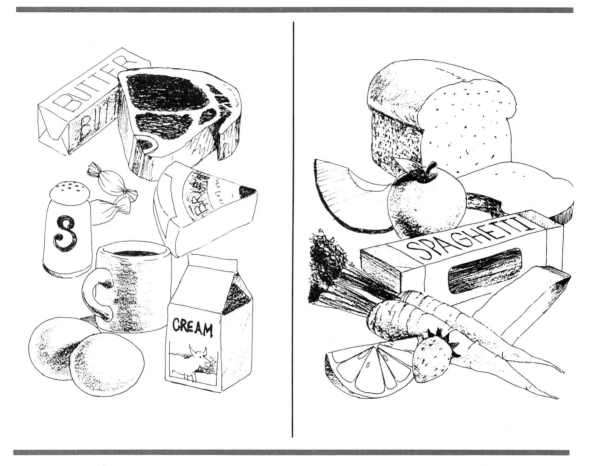

For most Americans, a healthier diet means eating less fat, cholesterol, salt, and protein (left side of diagram), and more complex carbohydrates such as grains, pasta, fruits, and vegetables (right side).

- Consume enough calcium. At least one-third of women consume less than half the calcium they need. Two to 3 glasses of milk or their equivalent in other calcium-rich foods are needed daily.

Although we have access to a great variety of nutritious foods, many of us eat too many foods that are high in calories but low in nutrients. To keep your diet in balance, follow the above guidelines along with these basic principles:

(continued on p. 64)

How Well Do You Eat?

Do you eat a well-balanced diet? Read the question and circle your answer, then tabulate your score at the end of the quiz.

1. I eat breakfast
   a. daily
   b. a couple of times a week
   c. rarely
2. For breakfast, I usually have
   a. juice, toast, tea, or coffee
   b. juice, cereal, and toast
   c. tea or coffee and a doughnut
   d. more than any of the above
   e. nothing
3. I regularly eat
   a. whole-grain bread
   b. white bread
   c. no bread at all
4. I have one glass of fruit juice, a grapefruit, an apple, an orange, or another fruit
   a. less than six times a week
   b. once a day
   c. two or more times a day
5. I drink a glass of milk
   a. once a day
   b. two or three times a day
   c. rarely
6. When I'm served fatty meat, I
   a. always trim off the fat
   b. often trim off the fat, but not always
   c. never trim off the fat
7. I have a salad or vegetable
   a. two or three times a week
   b. with two or more meals a day
   c. never
   d. with one meal a day
8. I eat fried foods
   a. two to three times a day
   b. two to five times a week
   c. about once a day
   d. rarely
9. I apply salt to my food
   a. in modest amounts when cooking, but never at the table
   b. sometimes, depending on the food
   c. almost always, it's a habit
   d. rarely or never
10. I have sweet desserts
    a. every day
    b. one to four times a week
    c. just on special occasions
11. I have snacks
    a. one or two times a week
    b. one or two times a day
    c. three or more times a day
12. I drink tea, coffee, or soft drinks
    a. six or more times a day
    b. less than twice a day
    c. two to six times a day
    d. rarely
13. I drink water by itself
    a. rarely
    b. less than one glass a day
    c. one to two glasses a day
    d. three or more glasses a day
14. I maintain a healthy weight by
    a. monitoring calories within my balanced diet
    b. fasting
    c. monitoring calories, as well as monitoring my exercise program
    d. trying many different diets
15. I eat at fast-food restaurants
    a. rarely
    b. two to four times a week
    c. every day
16. Complete this sentence: "Today I weigh. . .
    a. the same or less
    b. 1 to 15 pounds more
    c. 15 to 35 pounds more
    d. 35 pounds more
    . . . than I did when I was 21 years old."
17. I have alcoholic beverages
    a. almost daily, only 1 drink
    b. never
    c. daily, 1 to 2 drinks
    d. daily, 2 or more drinks

18. I consume fish
   a. two or three times a week
   b. rarely
   c. once a week

ANSWERS

1. *a = 3, b = 1, c = 0*   Score _____
Studies have found that people who eat breakfast have more energy and are more alert than those who don't.

2. *a = 2, b = 3, c = 1, d = 3, e = 0* Score _____
Your breakfast should contain at least three of the four food groups: a milk product, a bread or cereal, a fruit or vegetable, and an egg or piece of meat, fish, or poultry. Breakfast is a good time to eat a nutritious, high-fiber, low-fat meal.

3. *a = 3, b = 1, c = 0*   Score _____
Fiber, which is found in whole grains, may reduce blood cholesterol levels and the risk of colon cancer. Whole-grain breads are a good source of fiber.

4. *a = 0, b = 1, c = 3*   Score _____
Eat at least four to five servings of fruits, vegetables, or fruit juices a day for minerals, vitamins, and fiber.

5. *a = 1, b = 3, c = 0*   Score _____
Adult men should drink two glasses of milk or eat two servings of milk products a day. Women need three servings a day, while teens and pregnant women need four. Look for skim or low-fat products, which contain essential calcium without the extra fat. Calcium has been found to help reduce the risk of developing osteoporosis.

6. *a = 3, b = 1, c = 0*   Score _____
Eat two daily servings of meat, fish, poultry, or protein-alternatives, such as peanut butter or nuts. But be careful of the fat. Always trim off the fat from meats, because this is saturated fat, which has been shown to increase blood cholesterol levels. Most Americans eat twice as much protein as they need, and far too much fat.

7. *a = 1, b = 3, c = 0, d = 2*   Score _____
See answer 4. Fruits and vegetables not only are high in vitamins and minerals, but they also supply carbohydrates that fuel exercising muscles.

8. *a = 0, b = 2, c = 1, d = 3*   Score _____
Fried foods contain significantly more fat than broiled, baked, or steamed foods. If you fry foods, use polyunsaturated or monounsaturated oils, instead of saturated oils, lard, or hydrogenated vegetable oils.

9. *a = 3, b = 1, c = 0, d = 3*   Score _____
Americans consume much more salt than they need. And, some people who are salt-sensitive increase their blood pressure when they consume salt. Processed foods can contain a great deal more salt than foods prepared at home.

10. *a = 1, b = 2, c = 3*   Score _____
Eat sweets only if you have calories to spare. High-calorie desserts usually are high in fat and have few vitamins or other nutrients.

11. *a = 3, b = 2, c = 0*   Score _____
Snacks are not bad for you if you eat nutritious ones, such as fruits, vegetables, and whole-grain crackers. Yet snacking in excess leads to weight gain.

12. *a = 0, b = 2, c = 1, d = 3*   Score _____
Tea, coffee, and soft drinks have little or no nutritional value, yet contain caffeine, which can deplete the body of important nutrients if taken in excess.

13. *a = 0, b = 1, c = 2, d = 3*   Score _____
Water is vital for almost all body functions. The average person loses more than three liters of water a day, which must be replaced. Dehydration causes fatigue and a loss of coordination, and it can be fatal in extreme cases.

14. *a = 2, b = 0, c = 3, d = 0*   Score _____
Research has found that combining a healthy diet with exercise is the best way to lose or maintain weight. Dieting alone is not enough. Research also indicates that fasting and many fad diets are not only unhealthy, but also can, in fact, reduce your chance of reaching and maintaining a healthy weight.

15. *a = 3, b = 1, c = 0*   Score _____
Most of the food served at fast-food restaurants is high in calories, fat, and salt. Avoid eating regularly in fast-food restaurants. When you do, look for healthy selections, such as fruit juices, salads, or plain hamburgers on whole-wheat buns.

16. *a = 3, b = 2, c = 1, d = 0*   Score _____
Most people begin their adult years at a healthy weight but reduce their activity levels as they get older and slowly gain weight. People who are overweight have an increased risk of many diseases.

17. *a = 3, b = 3, c = 0, d = 1*   Score _____
Alcohol, along with smoking and caffeine, depletes the body's calcium supply and weakens bones. Alcohol also is high in calories but low in nutrients. And, it interferes with the body's absorption of several B vitamins. Research has shown, however, that consuming one serving of beer, wine, or hard liquor a day isn't harmful, and in fact is associated with a reduced risk of heart disease.

18. *a = 3, b = 0, c = 1*   Score _____
Eating cold-water fish, such as salmon, mackerel, and cod, has been found to help reduce blood cholesterol levels. In general, fish has less fat than red meat. Substitute fish for red meat two to three times a week.

WHAT YOUR SCORE MEANS

(45–54) You have excellent dietary habits. You seem to eat a balanced diet that includes generous portions from all four food groups.

(34–44) You have good dietary habits, but you could do better. Review your weakest areas and try to improve your diet.

(0–33) Your diet is inconsistent and unbalanced. Fitness is more than exercising and not smoking. Read a good book on diet or talk to a registered dietician. Don't just take vitamin supplements to try to overcome your poor dietary habits—it won't work.

By improving your diet—and by exercising regularly—you will be improving your health and enhancing your chances for a longer, happier life.

Source: Susan Kalish, *Running and Fitness,* Vol. 6, No. 11 (November 1988), pp. 4–5.

- Eat a variety of foods from different food groups to increase intake of a wide range of nutrients.
- Consume more unprocessed foods by choosing foods as close as possible to their farm-grown state (for example, an orange or orange juice instead of an orange-flavored fruit punch and whole wheat bread instead of enriched white bread).
- Emphasize protective foods. Whole grains rich in fiber and fruits and vegetables that are rich in vitamin C and beta-carotene (pro-vitamin A) protect against cancer; calcium-rich foods protect against osteoporosis and hypertension.
- Follow the principles of moderation and balance: eat the less nutritious foods less often and in smaller portions; eat the more nutritious foods more often and in greater quantity.
- Plan a diet of foods that you enjoy and make desired changes gradually.

(continued on p. 66)

Eating on the Run: Eat Often and Plan Ahead

Healthful eating intentions often get pushed aside in the course of a busy day. But eating on the run doesn't have to be a hazard of a harried schedule—if a few easy precautions are taken. Here's advice on how to manage eating on the run.

Tempting Pitfalls.

1. Attempting to save time by skipping meals will backfire. This "timesaving strategy" usually precipitates gorging in the form of a single large meal at the end of the day.

2. Relying solely on frozen dinners for good nutrition is a mistake. Most frozen entrees are not complete meals. They usually lack key vitamins such as A and C and are low in fiber. Be sure to include fresh fruits and vegetables as a part of meals.

3. Cutting back on supermarket shopping to save time will only leave kitchen cupboards bare, and cause a daily quandary over what to eat for dinner. Ironically, regular grocery shopping saves time by keeping cupboards stocked with all the essentials and eliminating the need for last minute trips for a missing ingredient.

Basic Survival.

1. Have a plan. If the day is overscheduled, plan easy snacks to help get through the day, rather than hoping to grab a bite somewhere.

2. Be sure to eat breakfast or a midmorning snack. Several studies have demonstrated that eating breakfast is key for optimal mental performance. Running on empty encourages brain drain.

3. Go no longer than five hours without eating. Prolonged hunger creates a one-track mind—the food track. You're likely to derail at the first sight of anything edible.

4. Graze—eat small snacks or mini-meals throughout the day. Nowhere is it written in stone that the only healthful way to eat is to have three meals a day. Just make sure to include the following each day, regardless of the number of meals you eat: two servings of low-fat dairy products, two servings of low-fat meats or dried beans and peas, five servings of fruits and vegetables and six servings of whole grain breads and cereals.

5. Don't rely on vitamin pills or supplements as a nutrition crutch. Americans' nutritional problem is not one of deficiencies, but rather excesses (too much fat and cholesterol). No vitamin supplement will resolve this problem.

Coping with Occupational Eating Hazards.

1. Long hours and unexpected meetings can easily cut into healthful eating plans, so be prepared. Stockpile the office refrigerator and your desk with easy, ready-to-eat snacks that are only a bite away:

Desk Snacks—mini-bagels, mini-boxes of raisins, pop-top tuna packed in water, low-fat crackers, boxed juices, durable fruit such as oranges, grapefruit, apples,or canned vegetable juice.

Refrigerator-Ready Snacks—nonfat or low-fat yogurts in 4- or 5-ounce snack size, low-fat cheeses (5 grams or less fat per ounce), nonfat or low-fat milk.

2. For healthful eating on the road, the best bet is to invest in a small portable cooler and bring healthful snacks and meals.

Making Meals in Minutes.

1. Use time-saving cooking methods such as one-dish recipes and microwave meals. Or let meals simmer in slow cooker while you're at the office.

2. Buy food pre-prepared, such as grated low-fat cheese, chopped produce from the salad bar, plain frozen vegetables and boneless, skinless chicken breasts. But be prepared to pay more for this convenience.

3. Keep quick staples on hand such as canned beans, water-packed tuna, frozen vegetables, turkey breast, spaghetti and canned pasta sauce, rice and lentils.

4. When you do have time to cook—take advantage and plan for leftovers. Double or triple the quantity of stew, for example, and freeze the leftovers for the future when time is more limited.

5. Round out frozen entrees with a serving of nonfat milk. Add a serving of whole grain pita, roll or crackers. Most frozen dinners and entrees provide small servings of vegetables or do not include them at all. So, pop frozen vegetables into the microwave to make the meal complete.

6. For ready-to-go salads try preparing a large batch of greens, cover with a paper towel and store in an airtight bowl. It should stay fresh for three to four days. Use as a dinner salad or make it a meal by adding tuna or leftover chicken. For a nutrition and fiber boost, add kidney or garbanzo beans.

7. Don't be afraid to have a cold meal such as a sandwich, salad and low-fat milk for dinner.

—Evelyn Tribole, M.S., R.D.

Source: *Environmental Nutrition*, February 1990, p. 2.

Food and Well-being

Eating well is important not only for preventing disease, but for improving daily energy level and endurance. For example, complex carbohydrate foods provide fuel for the nervous system and prevent fatigue. These foods are especially important for physically active people. Too much caffeine (found in coffee, black teas, and soft drinks) can add to feelings of stress and decrease energy level, as the nervous system is first stimulated by the caffeine and then depressed when the effect wears off. Some health experts recommend daily caffeine intake be kept to moderate levels, the amount in 2 or 3 cups of coffee.

Eating enough food and at regular intervals is also important. This might seem an obvious point, but surveys show that more than a quarter of Americans don't eat breakfast and almost a quarter skip lunch. [9] Skipping meals can increase fatigue and irritability and lead to poor nutrient intake, while regularly eating meals and healthy snacks (if desired) keeps one performing well mentally and physically. This is especially important during times when one is rushed and under stress—and most likely to let positive eating habits slide. Many people become anxious about their weight and restrict calories too much and for too long a period of time. Adequate caloric intake provides energy necessary for regular physical activity and, in the long run, aids weight loss more than severe calorie restriction.

Plan Ahead

In a society where most people have frequent access to foods high in fat and sugar (fast-food restaurants, vending machines, convenience stores, the corner doughnut shop), planning ahead becomes important. Consider which foods are available to you during the day that will meet your nutritional needs. If choices are limited, plan to bring snack foods along to school or work. If eating lunch frequently at restaurants is contributing too much fat to the diet, consider bringing a brown-bag lunch at least half of the time or seeking restaurants with better choices. (For more information about nutrition, see the book in this series entitled *Wellness: Nutrition & Health*.) [10]

COPING WITH STRESS

The fact that the tranquilizer Valium is one of the most frequently prescribed drugs in the country is, perhaps, an indication that many of us are ill-prepared to cope with the stresses of everyday life.

The body responds to stress with a number of physiological changes, including release of the hormone adrenalin into the blood and an increase in breathing, heart rate, blood pressure, and muscle tension. These changes, called the "fight-or-flight response," serve a useful purpose by readying the body to deal with a physical threat. Once the danger is dealt with, the body returns to a state of relaxation and lowered heart rate, blood pressure, and muscle tension.

Most of the stresses we face today, however, cannot be dealt with by fighting or running. They are **chronic** and ongoing stresses, often with no clear beginning and ending, rather than instances of physical danger necessitating a physical action. The body's response to these kinds of mental and physical pressures is less dramatic than the adrenalin-charged "fight-or-flight response," but, over time, chronic stress can lead to increased blood pressure and muscle tension, increased stomach acid secretion, excessive wear on the heart and arteries, and other harmful changes.

Rush-hour traffic, a consistently packed schedule of work and errands, a dispute with a co-worker, marital problems, a sick child, unpaid bills, hearing the 6 o'clock news—these are examples of ongoing background stresses that often occur simultaneously. If the body is not given a chance to reach a state of deep relaxation periodically, the result is stress exhaustion and increased susceptibility to stress-induced diseases, especially when a major stressful event occurs in addition to these background stresses.

Chronic: Term used to describe any disorder that persists over a long period of time; in contrast to acute.

Did You Know That . . .

There are several things you can do to help fight the negative effects of stress. They include eating a low-fat, low-cholesterol diet, exercising for 20 to 30 minutes a day at least 3 times a week, getting enough sleep, and avoiding obesity.

Becoming "Stress-hardy"

Stress can be categorized into three major areas:

- Cataclysmic events that are both major and unpredictable, such as war, floods, earthquakes, and the like.
- Major personal events, both predictable and unpredictable, such as an accident, a death, getting fired, getting married or divorced, or moving.
- Background events—daily hassles, frustrations, "hurry sickness," family problems, commuting, noise, and so forth.

Stress cannot be avoided completely, and some "positive" stress is even desirable. A certain amount of stress comes with any change. The new activities that bring interest and enjoyment to our lives challenge and push us to perform our best. But when clear signals of stress overload appear, stress levels need to be managed and reduced.

If positive coping skills are not present, negative ways of dealing with stress can develop, such as internalizing anger and other emotions, drinking, abusing drugs, arguing, eating poorly, and becoming ill or depressed. Positive coping skills, on the other hand, help one to stay healthy, fit and relaxed; to prepare mentally for anticipated stressful situations; to react less strongly to stressful situations; and to relax or heal more quickly when a major stress is over.

Physical Activity and Diet Exercise is one positive coping skill. Physical activity brings physiological changes to the body that directly counter the physical response to stress. Physical activity relaxes tense muscles, lowers blood pressure, dissipates stress hormones, renews mental energy, and brings relief from the day's frustrations. Aerobic types of exercise, such as a daily brisk walk, have been shown to be particularly effective in reducing stress.

Dietary habits also affect how stressed one feels. Excessive caffeine consumption can contribute to stress because caffeine stimulates stress hormones. Too few calories, too much sugar, or too few complex carbohydrates can contribute to low blood sugar, irritability, and fatigue. [11] A diet adequate in nutrients significantly helps the body to resist illness and infection.

Recreation and Leisure Do you need to be reminded to play? Making time for sports activities, camping, music, hobbies, reading, time with friends, and other interests brings enjoyment and

Symptoms of Stress Overload

Headaches
Back or shoulder pains
Jaw tension
Upset stomach or nausea
Constipation
Diarrhea
Heart pounding or erratic beat
Shortness of breath
Muscle tremors or tics
Change in appetite, up or down
Mood swings
Fatigue
Increased craving for tobacco, alcohol, drugs, or food

Allergy flare-up
Perspiration
Frequent colds
Skin rashes
Excessively dry skin or hair
Rapid or shallow breathing
Cold, sweaty hands
Asthma attack
Sexual dysfunction
Sleep difficulties
Anxiety and nervousness
Forgetfulness
Depression and apathy

balance to life. Such activities often take second place to work and family obligations as we grow older, but they are irreplaceable in fostering personal satisfaction. A **cardiologist** who has seen his patients succumb to heart attacks, caused in part by excessive stress and pressure to be financially successful, advises:

> You must look at your life and decide what is really important as a life goal. Concentrate on what you'd like to be, rather than on what you'd like to have. Understand and admit you can't accomplish everything. . . . Ask yourself how much of what you're doing is simply to conform to the pressures of society, your co-workers, your friends and your family. Keep in mind that your lifetime is limited. . . . If you don't like what you're doing, make changes so you're doing what you like. [12]

Specific Coping Skills Many specific stress management techniques can also contribute to stress reduction or bring relaxation after a tense encounter or a high-pressure day. Activities people find helpful include breathing exercises, techniques to relax muscles (**yoga**, stretching, massage, and progressive muscle relaxation), meditation or prayer, and visualization and imagery activities. These skills need to be learned and practiced over a period of time but, once learned, can provide immediate relax-

Cardiologist: A medical doctor who specializes in the diagnosis and treatment of disorders involving the heart.

Yoga: A system of exercises originating with the Hindu religion designed to promote control of the body and mind.

FIGURE 4.3
Choosing a Relaxing Activity

Taking time to enjoy sports, hobbies, and other relaxing activities can help reduce stress and bring balance into your life.

ation and benefit during stressful times. Time management training, developing assertiveness skills and the ability to say "no" to others when demands are too great, and obtaining counseling can all help reduce what may seem like an overwhelming level of stress and put life back into perspective and balance.

Stressful events themselves are less responsible for our stress level than the way that we *react* to them. You can minimize your reaction to stress through changes in life-style and attitude and by learning coping skills. Such changes reduce the impact of the unavoidable stresses on your health and well-being and help reduce or eliminate the many sources of stress over which you

FIGURE 4.4
Meditation

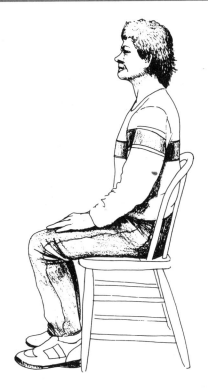

Many people have found meditation helpful as a means of reducing stress. An effective technique can be as simple as sitting in a comfortable position in a quiet room, breathing slowly and deeply, and focusing your attention on a single word, thought, or image.

have control. (More information about coping with stress is provided in the book in this series entitled *Wellness: Stress Management*.) [13]

SMOKING

"Quitting smoking is easy: I've done it a thousand times," said Mark Twain.

Over 75 percent of smokers say they want to quit the habit.

FIGURE 4.5
The Health Effects of Smoking

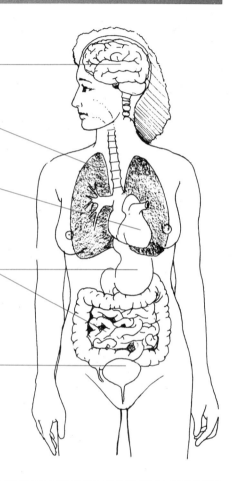

Brain: Smoking restricts oxygen flow and causes a narrowing of blood vessels in the brain, which can lead to stroke.

Lungs: Smoking increases the risk of lung cancer, the most deadly form of all cancers, and greatly increases the risk of emphysema, bronchitis, and pneumonia.

Heart and circulatory system: Smoking increases the heart rate, elevates blood pressure, constricts the blood vessels, and contributes to the buildup of fatty deposits in the arteries, greatly increasing the risk of heart disease. Smoking also reduces the level of oxygen in the blood, starving the body of oxygen.

Digestive tract: Carcinogens in cigarette smoke are a potential cause of cancer in any tissue with which they come in contact, including the mouth, throat, esophagus, stomach, and intestines. Smoking also increases secretion of digestive acids, increasing the risk of stomach and duodenal ulcers.

Bladder: Smoking increases the risk of cancer in the bladder, which stores and disposes of carcinogens that have been eliminated from the blood.

Female reproductive organs: Smoking increases the risk of cervical cancer. Pregnant women who smoke have an increased risk of miscarriage, premature birth, and infant mortality (not shown).

Smoking is always unhealthy. This illustration shows the parts of the body most affected by tobacco.

Many former smokers have quit "cold turkey" without any assistance, simply because they were ready and motivated. Quitting for many people, however, may require not just motivation and willpower, but learned skills. Most communities offer group smoking cessation programs that teach coping skills and guide quitters through the most difficult times. The American Lung

Association, the American Cancer Society, local hospitals, and private companies offer widely available programs. A guide to quitting on one's own is available from the American Lung Association (see Resources in appendix).

Two conditions have been shown to be essential to breaking the habit: truly having the desire to quit and having confidence in one's ability to quit. In other words, success is unlikely if someone is quitting because of outside pressure. The motivation must come from within. If not, the cycle of quitting and starting again can be vicious, significantly affecting one's self-confidence and leading to unnecessary guilt, anxiety, and lowered confidence in one's ability to quit in the future.

When a smoker is clearly ready and willing to quit, chances of success are very high. Some experts suggest that smokers who are not truly ready begin an exercise program instead. This not only helps counteract some of the ill effects of smoking, but it can lead to a greater desire to quit and less difficulty with withdrawal symptoms when the decision to quit is later reached.

Other authorities say most smokers will make more than one attempt to quit before they finally reach their goal. If one method does not work, try another. Different techniques help different people, and failure at one attempt does not mean that success is beyond reach in the future.

The smoker who quits gains significant health benefits. After 5 to 10 years, the risk of heart and lung disease decreases to a level comparable to that of people who have never smoked. Energy and a sense of well-being improve, and taste and smell sensations return to normal. Clothes, hair, car, and home stop smelling of smoke. Over 43 million Americans have quit since 1964 – 1.3 million people each year, a testament to the saying that "Where there's a will, there's a way." [14]

ALCOHOL AND DRUGS

In the movie *Postcards From the Edge,* Meryl Streep, playing the role of a would-be actress with a drug problem, laments languidly, "The problem with instant gratification is that it's not quick enough." Alcohol and drug use is an area more difficult to deal with than most life-style areas because our anything-goes social milieu and the short-term pleasures of use make drifting into potentially difficult straits all too easy. By the same token, careful observation of your own habits and behaviors related to these substances is crucial to your long-term well-being. You are

Did You Know That . . .

The United States produced over 1.4 billion pounds of tobacco in 1989.

the one who makes the ultimate choice when faced with a decision about use or abuse of a substance. Clear, insightful thinking about yourself and these substances, based on factual knowledge, is required to determine limits and guidelines with which you are comfortable.

Alcohol is an integral part of our culture. More than two-thirds of the adult population imbibes alcoholic beverages. One in 10 drinkers has a problem with alcohol, however. Its use is heavily promoted through advertising targeted particularly at college-age adults, blacks, Hispanics, and, most recently, women.

What are the facts? Occasional, moderate use of alcohol does not appear to impact negatively on health (except during pregnancy, when experts urge that even small amounts be avoided), but chronic overuse or acute abuse of alcohol clearly results in irreversible damage to the liver, stomach, spinal cord, and brain. Anyone who has experienced a hangover can testify to alcohol's short-term **toxic** effects and ability to alter behavior—this is not a substance that the body can handle easily.

The bad news about alcohol is familiar: in the long run, heavy alcohol use causes cancer, cirrhosis and other liver diseases, nutrition-related illnesses, nerve damage, destruction of brain cells, birth defects, fertility problems and impotence in men, and a host of other physical and mental problems. It damages relationships at home, with friends, and at work. [15] Not the least of the problems caused by alcohol is its substantial role in home and work accidents and in deaths on the highway— over half of motor vehicle accidents involve alcohol. [16]

How much alcohol is too much? In terms of physical health, averaging 2 drinks or less per day is generally considered "moderate use," with apparently little potential for health problems. Averaging 3 or more drinks a day is considered "heavy use." Research indicates that this level of drinking significantly increases the risk for potentially serious health problems.

Toxic: Term used to describe any substance known to produce harmful or poisonous effects upon exposure, usually through interference with one or more of the basic chemical reactions that take place in living tissues.

The reason why one drinks (or uses drugs) can determine whether such use creates another kind of problem. Alcohol can be used reasonably for relaxation and for cultural, religious, and social reasons. If it is routinely used to cope with anxiety or emotional hurt and to escape from worries, or is the only way to unwind or have a good time, an abuse problem may be present. If one's drinking habits are causing problems at home, at work, or anywhere else, it is time to take stock of the situation and make some hard decisions. [17]

Marijuana: The dried flower clusters and leaves of the Indian hemp plant that, when smoked or consumed, produce a euphoric alteration of mood.

Marijuana, although illegal, appears to be less toxic than our legal and more culturally accepted alcoholic beverages. It has

FIGURE 4.6
Harmful Effects of Cocaine

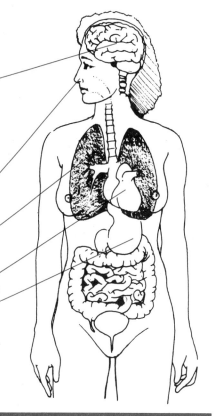

Brain and central nervous system: Cocaine stimulates the heat-regulating center of the brain causing hyperthermia (excessive body temperature), which kills brain cells. Cocaine also elevates blood pressure resulting in increased risk of stroke. High doses of cocaine can cause convulsions and tremors, which can shut down the central nervous sytem, cause respiratory failure, cardiac arrest, and death.

Nose: Inhaling cocaine can damage the lining of the nose, destroying the sense of smell.

Lungs: Smoking cocaine can damage the lungs and cause fluid buildup which reduces the body's supply of oxygen.

Heart and circulatory system: Cocaine can dramatically speed up the heart rate, which can result in fatal cardiac arrest. Anyone with a heart condition such as hypertension or cardiovascular disease is particularly vulnerable.

Stomach: Cocaine use can induce vomiting.

Cocaine affects the whole body and even small amounts can be fatal. This drawing shows some of the locations where cocaine is most likely to cause damage.

proven useful in treatment of glaucoma and in reducing the nausea associated with cancer **chemotherapy**. [18] As with alcohol, moderate use may not have any adverse effects on health or social functioning, but because of its illegal status, the body of research on marijuana is small. Marijuana is not completely benign, however. The active ingredient in marijuana, THC (tetrahydrocanabinol), is present in much higher concentrations in the marijuana grown today (6 percent) compared to 10 years ago (1–2 percent) and has been linked to short-term memory loss, lowered

Chemotherapy: Treatment involving the use of drugs or other medication designed to kill or reduce the growth rate of cancer cells.

sperm count, impaired immune response and heart function, and other problems. [19] Chronic marijuana use harms lung tissue just as tobacco use does. Research indicates long-term use also damages the nervous system, causes brain tissue to atrophy, and may cause genetic damage. [20]

Cocaine use has risen dramatically in recent years. Increasingly used for recreational purposes, cocaine also carries with it the risk of addiction and serious health consequences. Although widely regarded as harmless, it is, in fact, a powerful stimulant of the nervous system. It can cause a dangerously rapid heart beat and even death from sudden cardiac arrest. [21] This potential to cause sudden cardiac arrest is becoming more widely recognized. Athletes in top physical condition have succumbed, and medical researchers have suggested that the increasing availability in the United States of purer, less adulterated cocaine is responsible. In the long run, high blood pressure, harmful changes in sperm and brain tissue, death to fetuses, and birth defects can occur as well.

Although they receive the most media coverage, illegal drugs are only one category of misused drugs in our culture. Many over-the-counter or prescription medications meant to be used for short-term purposes or to treat a specific disease are abused, particularly tranquilizers, sleeping pills, and stimulants. Their potential to disrupt life, health, and well-being is no less than that of illegal drugs.

Although societal factors and influences we don't individually control may contribute to development of a substance abuse problem, it remains up to the individual to break the addictive cycle successfully and develop long-term solutions to the personal conditions that motivate substance abuse. This requires strong commitment and belief in one's self-worth. It may necessitate the help of a counselor or treatment program. (For more information on drugs and alcohol, see the book in this series entitled *Wellness: Drugs, Society, & Behavior.*) [22]

SAFETY

Cocaine: A white, crystalline drug obtained from the leaves of the South American cocoa plant that produces feelings of euphoria and increased energy when absorbed into the bloodstream; continued use of cocaine can lead to psychological dependence.

In chapter 3 it was stated that accidental injuries are the leading cause of death for people under age 45, with automobile accidents accounting for nearly half of the deaths and home accidents another third. An additional 15 percent of injuries occur on the job.

Alcohol is involved in the majority of accidental injuries. The risks of drinking and driving are widely known, but drinking and

Here are some common ways people rationalize not wearing a seat belt:

Notion: "If I wear a belt, I'll get trapped in the car and burn or drown."
Fact: In less than 1 percent of automobile accidents does the car burn or become submerged in water. And in those few accidents a seat belt will most likely save you from becoming knocked unconscious so that you will be *more* likely to escape.

Seat Belt Myths

Notion: "In an accident, it's safer to be thrown free of the car."
Fact: If you are thrown from the car by a collision, you are 25 times more likely to be killed than if you remain strapped in the car.

Notion: "I always drive slowly, so even if I'm in an accident, it will just be a fender bender."
Fact: When not wearing seat belts, people have been killed at speeds as low as 8 to 12 miles an hour.

Notion: "People die wearing seat belts, too; I'll take my chances."
Fact: Over your lifetime, you have a one in three chance of being seriously injured in a car accident. The odds of being killed are far less if a seat belt is worn. A lap/shoulder seat belt cuts the odds of dying by 57 percent, a lap belt alone, 31 percent. One-third of serious injuries are caused by passengers colliding with the windshield or steering wheel and another 25 percent of serious injuries are due to passengers colliding with each other. Seat belts can prevent this.

Did You Know That . . .

Extensive research has found that rear seat belts in automobiles can reduce the incidence of serious injury and death by about 40 percent.

operating machinery or drinking and walking are also risky—40 percent of pedestrians killed by automobiles are drunk.

Injury rates in the United States remain exceptionally high in spite of the fact that most accidents are preventable. One observer states, "It is a question of will rather than way. We are not waiting for any fundamental discovery or new drug or new technology. We are waiting for ourselves." [23]

THE MIND AND WELL-BEING

Do our mind and mental attitudes influence physical health? Do our physical habits affect our mental health? In recent years, numerous connections between mind and body have been newly identified.

Opiate: Any drug derived from or chemically similar to opium, a drug prepared from the unripened pods of the opium poppy; a narcotic.

Endorphins: A group of substances formed within the body that relieves pain.

Narcotic: Any drug that dulls the senses or induces sleep and may produce dependence if used for a prolonged interval, especially the class of drugs derived from the opium poppy.

Morphine: An opium derivative that relieves pain while producing a euphoric state; prolonged use can lead to dependence.

Placebo: A chemically inert substance administered in place of a drug. The benefit gained from taking a placebo occurs because the patient believes it will have a positive effect.

Catecholamines: Hormones, including adrenaline (epinephrine), that are released from the adrenal glands as part of the body's stress response; these substances serve to stimulate the body and prepare it for action.

Running can increase the secretion of natural, **opiate**-like chemicals in the brain. Called **endorphins**, they are thought to be responsible for the "high" many runners experience. Endorphins, produced in the spinal cord and brain, also serve as some of the body's natural painkillers. They are thought to act by inhibiting pain impulses in certain centers of the brain. Chemically similar **narcotic** drugs, such as **morphine**, reduce pain through this same mechanism. [24] Exercise has been shown to improve mood considerably and to lower levels of anxiety, confusion, fatigue, and tension. [25]

Interestingly, since the 1950s scientists have been finding that a **placebo** (an inactive medication, such as a sugar pill) administered to patients under the guise that it is an effective drug will bring pain relief in 30 to 40 percent of patients with such conditions as migraine, angina, ulcer, coughing, and seasickness. This does not mean the patients who were helped by the "placebo effect" were suffering from a problem that was feigned or "psychological" in origin, but rather that the anticipation and belief that a treatment will work actually produce biochemical changes in the body, including, scientists think, the production of endorphins. Nor does there seem to be a "placebo personality" – placebos can work for anybody in the right circumstances. [26]

"A merry heart doeth good like a medicine: but a broken spirit drieth the bones" (the Book of Proverbs). Norman Cousins, the former editor of *Saturday Review*, claimed that laughter helped him recover from an incurable, degenerative spinal condition. In constant pain, he discovered that after watching Marx Brothers movies and old *Candid Camera* shows he could get an hour of pain-free sleep. Although the medical community was skeptical at the time, later research has uncovered evidence that laughter helps heal, and possible explanations for how laughter diminishes pain have been explored. A thigh-slapping guffaw has been shown to lower blood pressure, increase respiration and oxygenation, relax muscles, and reduce stress. Laughter also stimulates hormones called **catecholamines**, which in turn stimulate endorphin production, a potential link between laughter and pain reduction. [27] While medical science continues to investigate the reasons behind the benefit, it is important to keep your sense of humor!

Optimism and a sense of control over life's events contribute to well-being and longevity. A state of "learned helplessness," in which individuals feel hopeless and as if they do not have control over events or stresses in their lives, is associated with poor health outcomes. How does one "learn" to be helpless? Children

(continued on p. 80)

The medical community laughed in 1976 when Norman Cousins, the former editor of *Saturday Review* and now adjunct professor of medical humanities at the School of Medicine at UCLA, claimed that humor had helped him recover from a degenerative spinal condition. Watching Marx Brothers movies and segments of Candid Camera, Cousins claimed that 10 minutes of belly laughing got him an hour of pain-free sleep. Laughter, observed Cousins, caused the muscles of the abdomen, chest, shoulders, and elsewhere to contract, and heart rate, respiration rate, and blood pressure to increase. After laughter, Cousins said, muscles are more relaxed than before; heart rate and blood pressure dip below normal. "Inner jogging," he called it.

Laughing Toward Longevity

Since Cousins made his apparently silly claim, physicians have done some serious research on the subject. And indeed they have reached delightful conclusions. According to Dr. William Fry of Stanford, laughter increases respiratory activity, oxygen exchange, muscular activity, and heart rate; it stimulates the cardiovascular system, sympathetic nervous system, **pituitary gland,** and production of hormones called catecholamines—which in turn stimulate the production in the brain of endorphins, the body's natural pain-reducing enzymes and the chemical cousins to morphine and heroin. The production of beta-endorphins may cause "runner's high"—and may similarly cause "laugher's high."

It may seem farfetched to suppose that an occasional guffaw can have beneficial cardiovascular effects the way jogging can. But in a real physiological way it may reduce stress, hypertension, and thus depression, heart attacks, and strokes. It can possibly be, as the psychologist Jeffrey Goldstein of Temple University has said, that laughter "is related in several ways to longevity."

People start laughing early in life. Infants start laughing about the tenth week after birth, usually simply in reaction to such sensations as bowel movements or passing gas. By the sixteenth week they are laughing about once an hour. And by age four the little comedians are laughing about once every four minutes.

Certainly a good, old-fashioned thigh-slapper can be a real workout, raising body temperature about half a degree, setting the whole cardiovascular system pulsating, throwing the abdominal, lumbar, internal intercostal, subcostal, and transverse thoracic muscles into gear, rocking the glottis and larynx, rumbling up the windpipe, and banging against the trachea to emerge, finally, in a burst of mirth that sometimes issues from a person at a speed of 70 miles an hour, followed by muscle relaxation.

Recently, in research carried out by the Laughter Project at the University of California at Santa Barbara, it was found that laughter did

Did You Know That . . .

Although your blood pressure goes up during hearty laughter, from a normal systolic pressure of 120 to as high as 200, it drops to normal afterward and helps to release stress.

Pituitary gland: A small, pea-sized gland located at the base of the brain that regulates and controls the activity of the other endocrine glands (glands that release hormones directly into the bloodstream).

as well in reducing stress as more complex **biofeedback** training programs did. And laughter, as the researchers pointed out, requires no special training, no special equipment, and no special laboratory atmosphere. All it requires is a funny bone.

Source: *University of California Berkeley Wellness Letter,* Vol. 1, No. 9, June 1985, p. 1.

who grow up in authoritarian families may learn to be passive and acquiescent and carry these traits to adulthood, with an adverse effect on health. Some authorities believe when the parenting strategy is "do what I tell you, and don't ask why," and noncompliance is treated with punishment rather than explanation, children don't learn to cope effectively or to control their reaction to stressful situations. Instead, they develop helplessness and resignation. On the other hand, children who are encouraged to accept challenges and who learn that their actions make a difference develop successful coping strategies and the ability to implement beneficial changes in their lives later. This positive attitude alone has a powerful effect on recovery from illness and other stressful events. [28] Some observers think our system of medical care fosters "learned helplessness" by removing control of daily routines from hospital patients and by unwittingly fostering a "medical mystique" that leads people to feel they can't understand or determine the best course of medical intervention or nonintervention for themselves. [29]

Physical environment also affects mental well-being. Seasonal Affective Disorder (SAD), due to decreased sunlight during winter causes "wintertime blahs"–depression, sleep difficulties, and fatigue. Scientists theorize that SAD results from increased secretion of a hormone called melatonin. Daily exposure to sunlight or special lights in the home can bring remarkable improvement. [30]

Self-esteem is also intimately tied to health. A study of 204 men over 4 decades, from adolescence through middle age, found that those with poor emotional adjustment, chronic anxiety, and depression experienced greater physical deterioration with age and more adverse health consequences. [31]

In many cases, it is unclear from where benefit derives–do healthier people feel more optimistic or does feeling more optimistic lead to improved health and longevity? It probably works both ways–the mind and body constantly interact with each other. By making changes in one aspect of ourselves, we bring changes to the other. W

Biofeedback: A method of learning to control bodily functions by monitoring one's own muscle tension, skin temperature, and brain waves.

5

Wellness and Society

HEALTH AND WELL-BEING are not determined by personal life-style habits alone, but also by the interactions between ourselves and others, the environment of which we are a part, and the norms, habits, and values of our society. The loneliness and isolation an elderly person in a nursing home feels, the smog that blankets city streets, and the changes in the pace of life and physical activity that come with an automobile-dependent culture are examples of conditions that profoundly affect health and well-being. By becoming aware of how such factors affect us, we can make choices that improve our own health, the well-being of those around us, and the state of our environment.

FRIENDSHIP, INTIMACY, AND SHARING

The individual exists in the center of a vast social network—family, intimate friends, acquaintances, coworkers, and neighbors. Included in this network may be one's church, other organizations, social groups, counselors, and health professionals serving as sources of support, advice, and sharing. Research has shown that one's level of **social support**, as this network of many relationships is termed, is a significant factor in the ability to resist the effects of severe stress, in preventing disease, and in recovering from illness.

Social Support Networks
Humans are social animals and experience pain, anxiety, and depression when too isolated or alone. The simple experience of companionship can speed recovery in an ill person. A depressed mental state and negative attitude are known to prolong recovery

Social support: The psychological, emotional, and other forms of support provided by spouse, family members, relatives, friends, acquaintances, and community ties.

from illness, while a positive attitude, fostered by the presence of family and friends, enhances recovery, probably through complex interactions between the brain and the **immune system**.

Studies have shown that people with few friends and social contacts have increased mortality from heart disease, cancer, suicide, and accidental death. [1] On the other hand, those who belong to a church or other organization are healthier than those who do not. [2] Women tend to have more close friends with whom they share feelings and find support than men do, and several studies have linked reduced rates of illness in women with their greater social support networks. [3] Even when other life-style and health factors are examined, the relationship between having a strong network of social support and experiencing better health is clear—whether the support comes from family, close friends, friends with whom a common interest is shared, church, or other social memberships. [4]

What accounts for this greater resistance to illness and disease experienced by people with strong support networks? It is not clear whether those with more social contacts develop better self-esteem and more confidence in themselves (factors that lead to a more positive outlook on life and less perceived stress) or whether healthier people are simply more likely to seek out friendships. Do people with strong social support networks feel more comfortable with themselves and trust others more? One researcher has proposed that trust in others is a major factor in lowered levels of stress in modern society compared to premodern society and that this accounts for lower disease rates. Severely stressful events, such as the death of a spouse or a divorce, are associated with illness. Do social networks promote health by buffering individuals during times of stress? These are questions being explored in the field of social support research.

Without knowing the mechanism, however, it is clear that having one or more persons with whom one experiences emotional intimacy, talks openly, finds acceptance, and shares pleasurable companionship is a major factor in both mental and physical well-being.

Family Well-being
Family characteristics are a strong influence on the individual's health and ability to cope with stressful life events. In addition to learning life-style habits from parents, children acquire (to a large extent) their values, attitudes, beliefs, and sense of self-worth from them, factors that are intimately connected to every aspect of well-being and life satisfaction.

Immune system: The body's natural defense system, which works to eliminate pathogens.

FIGURE 5.1
Sharing with Friends

Did You Know That . . .

With our modern, mobile society family members can become scattered more readily, and thus an emotional support group in times of stress is lost. Devoted friendships become that much more important for those who move away from their family members.

A strong social support system including friends, family, coworkers, and other important people in your life can be a significant factor in reducing stress, preventing disease, and speeding recovery from illnesses.

Emotionally healthy families have less stressed, healthier members. Within the healthy family an individual finds a place for rest and recuperation from outside stresses and an atmosphere that is supportive and nonjudgmental. The family also serves as a sounding board and reference point when individuals face problems and conflicts of values in their lives. Families provide reassurance and support during periods of doubt and crisis. Families may also be a source of practical aid during day-to-day activities and hard times, whether through financial support, assistance with chores, or help with babysitting. Families participate in the celebration of special events. For many people, close friends also serve in some of these roles.

Family characteristics, in fact, are thought to be a good predictor of how an individual responds to the stresses in his or

(continued on p. 85)

Characteristics of Effective Families

1. *They have a chief;* that is, there is someone around whom other family members cluster.

2. *They have a switchboard operator;* that is, there is someone who keeps track of what all the others are up to.

3. *They are much to all their members but everything to none;* that is, family members are encouraged to be involved with and have some of their needs met by people outside of the family.

4. *They are hospitable;* that is, they recognize that hosts need guests as much as guests need hosts, and they maintain a surrounding of honorary family members. These "guests" become additional support systems for family members.

5. *They deal squarely with direness;* that is, when trouble comes— and in family life occasional trouble is unavoidable—it is dealt with quickly and openly, and is not allowed to threaten family bonds.

6. *They prize their rituals;* that is, they observe holidays together, grieve at funerals together, and in other ways encourage a sense of continuity and connectedness.

7. *They are affectionate;* that is, family members hug, kiss, and shake hands. They are quick to demonstrate love and caring for one another.

8. *They have a sense of place;* that is, there is a house or a town or some other place to which they feel connected. Even families who have moved often can feel connected to the place in which they presently find themselves.

9. *They connect with posterity;* that is, family members feel as though something came before them and something will continue when they die to which they are linked.

10. *They honor their elders;* that is, grandparents and other elderly relatives are respected and cared for. Their experience and wisdom—and they themselves—are valued.

Source: Jane Howard, *Families* (New York: Simon & Schuster, 1978), pp. 268–273.

One observer of families, author Jane Howard, found that effective families share some or all of the characteristics described above.

her life. Studies during the Depression showed that family integration, adaptability, and marital adjustment were key factors in how well a family coped with crisis. [5] People who are married have lower mortality rates than those who are single, divorced, or widowed. [6] Particularly for men, marriage appears to provide a source of psychological support and comfort that is associated with lower disease rates. [7]

Just as a healthy, supportive family seems to confer greater health on its members, a family that functions poorly and in which tension exists increases the likelihood of illness. Mental health problems, diabetes, the eating disorder **anorexia nervosa**, and **asthma** in children have all been linked to families in which parents are experiencing tension between themselves and draw their children into the conflict. [8]

Although we often assume the individual alone is the determinant of his or her health, the attitudes, coping skills, and emotional foundation derived from the family, both during childhood and adulthood, have a significant impact.

Pets

Anyone who has had a pet can testify to the strong emotional attachment that develops. In addition to being a "best friend," pets have been shown to improve mental health in the elderly, reduce fear and anxiety in children in stressful situations, and improve recovery in heart patients. [9] The health benefits are thought to result from the presence of a trusting, nonjudgmental, and affectionate companion, another source of social support. People own pets because they enjoy them, and they don't need medical reports to justify the pet's niche in the household. However, the evidence that pets may be especially beneficial to those whose lives have been interrupted by illness or loss illustrates again the significant effect of warm, affectionate companionship—even the whiskered, four-legged variety—on well-being.

WELLNESS AT THE WORK SITE

For much of the population, the majority of waking hours are spent in the workplace, and its health or hazard level can have a major impact on individual health. Exposure to dangerous chemicals and conditions on the job are regulated by government agencies, although funding cuts over the last decade have reduced enforcement of safety standards considerably. Noise level, exposure to **sidestream cigarette smoke**, poor ventilation, desk

Did You Know That . . .

The most common household pets are dogs and cats. Among pure breeds, there are 50 registered dog breeds and 27 registered cat breeds.

Anorexia nervosa: An eating disorder characterized by refusal to eat that can lead to extreme loss of weight, hormonal disturbances, and even death.

Asthma: An abrupt or chronic condition characterized by narrowed airways within the lungs that significantly obstruct airflow and cause difficulty in breathing.

Sidestream smoke: The smoke that escapes from the tip of the cigarette without being inhaled by the smoker.

You work in a factory.

Your day begins at 7:30 A.M. You arrive on time and cheerfully greet your fellow workers. At the sound of a small whistle, you take your place—and begin a twenty-minute session of stretching and limbering exercises. At 8 o'clock you head for the assembly line, fresh, invigorated, alert.

Wellness in the Factory

At mid-morning, you take a short break, then join your quality control circle. You talk about your line's productivity, about possible improvements, about any potential new policies that might be forthcoming from management. Then back to work.

At noon, you eat a moderate, nutritious lunch, then head out to the athletic area for a quick game of tennis, volleyball or softball. After a ninety-minute break, you return to the line.

Sound like another world? It's not. It's simply a picture of everyday worklife in Japan. It's no coincidence that productivity in Japan is increasing at 10 percent a year, while productivity in the United States has been declining.

The enlightenment of Japanese business management with regard to employee health may well have significant implications for workers in this country. American corporate executives, who are making jet-age pilgrimages to the Asian Mecca of productivity, are returning from Japan with new-found respect for the importance of employee health and fitness. No matter what the product, good health is good business.

Source: Charles Jennings and Mark J. Tager, "Good Health Is Good Business," *Medical Self-Care* (Summer 1981), p. 17.

jobs that promote back problems, and tedious machine operation that causes muscle and skeletal problems are additional conditions that affect health. People also report that a large portion of their life stress is related to concerns about job performance, work load, problems with supervisors or coworkers, and nonsupportive organizational policies.

Employee wellness programs are now promoted in thousands of businesses as a way to improve the health and productivity of employees and to reduce the employer's substantial health-care costs. The programs aim to prevent disease and illness and to reduce costs of treatment when problems do develop. The medical bill for American companies is more than $700 billion a year and is now the second largest expense of doing business.

Employee wellness programs often include preventive health services such as cancer, cholesterol, and blood pressure screening. Programs may provide educational programs about exercise, nutrition, weight management, and stress management, with rewards to employees who participate in such activities. Companies who offer well-planned wellness programs have saved large amounts of money through substantial reductions in absenteeism and medical costs, and improvements in employee health, morale, and productivity.

Programs to help the estimated 15 percent of workers who have alcohol problems are also offered by many businesses. Called Employee Assistance Programs, they provide counseling and referral to alcohol or drug treatment programs and have proven very effective in improving people's lives, saving employers money, and reducing the high rates of work-site injuries related to alcohol.

Workplaces are an ideal place for people to learn about positive life-style practices, since cost-effective group programs can be offered. The fact that services are provided at work makes participation convenient. For working parents, who may commute long distances to work, drop off and pick up children from day-care centers in the morning and evening, and return home to chores and meal preparation, convenience of programs is a necessity. The continuing trend among larger companies to offer employee wellness programs indicates they are perceived by business managers as ultimately cost-effective and valuable services.

AGING

Aging and death are the consequences of living and are natural stages of life. The distorted way in which our society looks on aging and the elderly, however, exerts a powerful and harmful influence on how we treat old people and how we view our own aging. We tend to think of older people as deficient in intellect, tiresome to talk to, weak, docile, asexual, and inactive—all unfounded **stereotypes**. The poor treatment of older persons in our society causes a fear of aging, an anxiety and stress that can actually accelerate the aging process. Even though a person is less strong than when younger, this does not mean he or she must become inactive, kept out of the mainstream of family and community activity, denied opportunities, or treated with disrespect.

With age, several physiological changes take place, including

Did You Know That . . .

The typical 40-year-old man who does not exercise, fails to wear a seat belt, smokes 2 packs of cigarettes a day, and is 30 percent overweight costs his employer over $1,500 a year in medical bills, double the nearly $750 spent on someone the same age with a healthier life-style.

Stereotype: A popular but oversimplified and inaccurate perception or belief.

a slowing of metabolic rate and a decrease in muscle tone, immune function, lung capacity, and pumping ability of the heart. Bones may become brittle, hair may be lost, and the senses of hearing, sight, taste, smell, and touch may diminish.

Many of these physical changes also occur in inactive people of any age, and researchers now believe several of the health changes associated with aging can be prevented or slowed by remaining active throughout life. For example, muscle tone, metabolic rate, lung and heart function, and bone strength can all be improved in older people who begin a regular exercise program. [10]

Although life expectancy of those who reach adulthood has increased a few years during the last century, there is evidence that more people now spend their later years in a debilitated state, dependent on drugs and medical intervention. Medical science can treat diseases and prolong survival, but the debilitation and physical limitation of living with a disease severely limit enjoyment of life. Maintaining a healthy life-style may extend life, but, more important, it ensures that one has the energy and stamina to enjoy the later years and have them be as fulfilling and interesting as earlier years—perhaps even more so.

A large study of adults in Alameda County, California, found that older people with good life-style habits were as healthy as people 30 years younger with poorer life-style habits. [11] The international Senior Olympics event is a testament to the vigor, enjoyment, and health one can have in older years—many athletes who participate in the rigorous competitive events of the Senior Olympics are in their 70s or older and did not become involved in sports until their later years. Here, the maxim "use it or lose it" clearly applies.

The saying "you are as young as you feel" also has much truth to it. The best health is attained by those who, as they age, strive to remain physically active, maintain ties of intimacy and friendship, and continue with intellectual interests. [12]

Dying
Fear of the unknown often produces anxiety in people, and fear of death is no exception. Many people fear becoming old and dying just as they fear other unknowns—traveling to a foreign country, moving to a new town, or leaving college to find a job, for example. If one ignores the fear and pretends it doesn't exist, the fear only becomes more difficult to cope with as the feared situation looms closer.

Because in our society death and dying are not dealt with
(continued on p. 90)

"They say an old man is twice a child," Shakespeare wrote in *Hamlet,* and the notion that our minds inevitably weaken with age is still widely shared. But experts are finding that just the reverse is often true: a decline in mental abilities is not inevitable. Many abilities once thought to wither do not, and some actually improve with age.

For example, age really does breed wisdom. Among the traits that improve in healthy older people is what psychologists call "crystallized intelligence"—using past experience to evaluate a situation or a problem for which there is no correct answer, such as assessing a political debate. According to Dr. John Horn, a psychologist at the University of Denver, this ability keeps growing at least through a person's sixties.

Keeping the Mind Fit

Another mental advantage gained with age is in how we use our knowledge. Drs. Janet Lachman and Roy Lachman at the University of Houston found that older people who are free of certain debilitating diseases tend to draw more efficiently on "world knowledge"—the immense store of factual and practical information built up over a lifetime. They also appear to have a more realistic sense of what they are and are not capable of. Both these traits can make them better able to cope with new situations.

What does fall off is "fluid intelligence," which helps us learn new processes and relationships—calculating math problems, for instance, or learning to use a computer. But this doesn't mean we lose the ability to learn. It simply takes us longer. What allows us to retain our mental powers is the brain itself. A healthy brain does not, as many people believe, lose multitudes of cells as a person ages.

The work of these and other experts convincingly suggests that as people age they can take steps to maintain their mental abilities. The principal requirement is to be mentally active. A mind, like a muscle, goes slack without exercise—and for many people, their job is their main mental exercise. After retirement, therefore, people should "tone" their minds. Reading widely is an excellent way to achieve this. Other good mind conditioners are hobbies, adult education courses, and active games like Scrabble and bridge. An active social life is also important, and so is being open, not rigid, in your attitudes and behavior. Finally, too many people have negative images of growing old. You can counter this by finding a positive role model—a vital older person who is living proof that at 70, 80, or 90 you can be sharper than ever.

Source: *University of California Berkeley Wellness Letter,* Vol. 1, No. 11, August 1989, p. 4.

Did You Know That . . .

Many people remain productive in their old age. Verdi composed his *Ave Maria* at age 85, Michelangelo was carving the *Rondanini Pieta* six days before he died at age 89, and the late Dr. Seuss continued writing into his 80s.

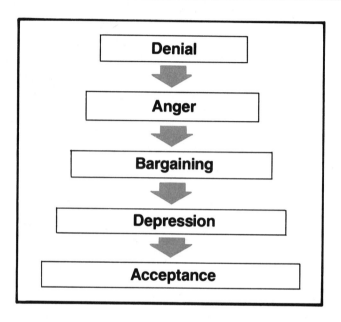

FIGURE 5.2
Kübler-Ross's Stages of Dying

Elizabeth Kübler-Ross proposed that many terminally ill people go through 5 different stages as they prepare to die.

openly and frankly, people's fears and concerns remain unaddressed. Elisabeth Kübler-Ross, a noted speaker and counselor on death and dying, believes that people can become comfortable with the thought of their own death by consciously spending time confronting their fears and dealing with the reality of death. Spiritual beliefs and seeing a continuity of existence after death are a source of inner strength and peace for many, but each individual must resolve his or her feelings about death in a way that feels right for him or her.

The use of medical technology to extend life at the expense of quality of life is of concern to many people who fear a prolonged illness and dependency on others. Formally stating one's wishes regarding this can reduce anxiety. A **living will** is a document that states, for the benefit of physician and family, one's wishes

Living will: A statement of personal instructions outlining the measures of heroic medical care (particularly life-support systems) desired and not desired by an individual, should that individual become incapacitated and unable to make decisions.

(continued on p. 92)

[In] December [1990] the U.S. Supreme Court heard opening arguments in *Cruzan v. The State of Missouri,* the suit filed by the parents of Nancy Cruzan, a 31-year-old woman rendered brain dead in a car crash seven years ago and kept alive in a hospital with the aid of a feeding tube. The parents argue that life support should be removed, since their daughter would not want to live in an irreversible coma. The state insists that life support be maintained. The case is complicated by the fact that Nancy Cruzan left no living will or other statement of her wishes.

Why You Need a Living Will

Under the law of most states, a patient has the right to choose—or refuse—any treatment. But when the patient cannot express his wishes, important decisions are left up to family members, doctors, hospital administrators, and—if conflict should arise—courts of law. Such tangles may be greatly simplified if the patient in question has, in advance, expressed his wishes in writing and left instructions for carrying these out.

A living will specifies which treatments you would or would not want if you were to become irreversibly incapacitated and dependent on life-sustaining treatment. Some living-will forms simply state that you would refuse "heroic" treatment. But you can also specify when you would or would not want cardiac resuscitation, a mechanical respirator, or a feeding tube. You can ask for painkilling drugs, or to be allowed to die at home. Living wills are not legally binding, but 40 states now have "right-to-die" laws, which often recognize living wills as good evidence of intent, and Congress may soon require all states to recognize them as such.

You can get a living-will form that already spells out the basics; you fill in the particulars according to your convictions (see Fig. 5.3). Remember that these forms have limitations, including lack of flexibility, in some cases, and ambiguous language. If there's no place in the form for you to fill in particulars, attach a page. State your terms as clearly as possible. For example, be precise about conditions—such as "irreversible brain damage that makes me unable to swallow"—under which you would or wouldn't want extraordinary measures to be taken on your behalf. No matter how explicitly you communicate your wishes, though, it's virtually impossible to anticipate every situation. You do not need a lawyer to make a living will—though legal advice may certainly prove useful.

In some states (for example, California and New York) a living will should be backed up with a Durable Power of Attorney for Health Care (DPAHC). This legally binding document empowers a designated person to make health-care decisions on your behalf. Choose someone to whom you've thoroughly explained your beliefs and who shares your philosophical position or at least clearly understands it. (You'll also need a back-up, in case your first choice is unable to act for you.) This person will have the authority to see that your wishes are carried out.

None of us is exempt from calamity or serious illness: everybody needs a living will and, if required, a DPAHC. The elderly, the chronically ill, and anyone about to undergo major surgery should certainly execute these documents. **Most important:** no document can substitute for frank discussions with your family, doctor, religious adviser, or friends who might be directly involved if you were critically ill. Besides ensuring that your wishes will be honored, a comprehensive living will and a DPAHC may help your family through some tough decisions.

Living-will essentials

- Sign the document before two witnesses—neither of whom should be a potential heir or the attending doctor, nurse, or health-care-facility employee. In some states living wills and DPAHCs must be notarized. Your surrogate can be your heir or spouse or anyone you select.
- Give copies to your immediate family, doctor, and anyone else involved. Don't store these documents in a safe deposit box or other inaccessible place. To be useful, they must be available.
- To keep your documents legally binding, repeat signing and, if necessary, notarization every couple of years.

Source: *University of California Berkeley Wellness Letter,* Vol. 6, No. 6, March 1990, pp. 1–2.

---

regarding implementation of medical measures should one become incapacitated and unable to make decisions regarding health or survival. The growing **hospice** movement in industrialized countries is another response to the "medicalization of death." Hospice care facilities and services are dedicated to providing a supportive, comfortable environment for people in the last weeks or months of life.

WELLNESS IN A TECHNOLOGICAL SOCIETY

Hospice: A facility where care is provided to terminally ill individuals.

Machines and electronic devices have become commonplace in industrialized, consumer-oriented nations. Most advances in technology come with a hidden price. No one can deny the convenience that cars provide, yet the increasingly sedentary life-style they foster is a clear risk factor for major disease, and the

(continued on p. 94)

FIGURE 5.3
A Living Will

INSTRUCTIONS	
Consult this column for guidance.	To My Family, Doctors, and All Those Concerned with My Care

This declaration sets forth your directions regarding medical treatment.

I, _____, being of sound mind, make this statement as a directive to be followed if I become unable to participate in decisions regarding my medical care.

If I should be in an incurable or irreversible mental or physical condition with no reasonable expectation of recovery, I direct my attending physician to withhold or withdraw treatment that merely prolongs my dying. I further direct that treatment be limited to measures to keep me comfortable and to relieve pain.

You have the right to refuse treatment you do not want, and you may request the care you do want.

These directions express my legal right to refuse treatment. Therefore I expect my family, doctors, and everyone concerned with my care to regard themselves as legally and morally bound to act in accord with my wishes, and in so doing to be free of any legal liability for having followed my directions.

You may list specific treatment you do not want. For example: Cardiac resuscitation Mechanical respira-tion Artificial feeding/ fluids by tube Otherwise, your gen-eral statement, top right, will stand for your wishes.

I especially do not want: _____
_____
_____
_____
_____

You may want to add instructions or care you do want—for ex-ample, pain medication; or that you prefer to die at home if possible.

Other instructions/comments: _____
_____
_____
_____

Proxy Designation Clause: Should I become unable to communicate my instructions as stated above, I designate the following person to act in my behalf:

Name: _____

Address: _____

If the person I have named above is unable to act on my behalf, I authorize the following person to do so:

Name: _____

Address: _____

If you want, you can name someone to see that your wishes are carried out, but you do not have to do this.

This Living Will Declaration expresses my personal treatment preferences. The fact that I may have also executed a document in the form recommended by state law should not be construed to limit or contradict this Living Will Declaration, which is an expression of my common-law and constitutional rights.

Sign and date here in the presence of two adult witnesses, who should also sign.

Signed: _____ Date: _____

Witness: _____ Witness: _____

Address: _____ Address: _____

_____   _____

Keep the signed original with your personal papers at home. Give signed copies to doctors, family, and proxy. Review your Declaration from time to time; initial and date it to show it still expresses your intent.

Source: Society for the Right to Die.

A living will is a document that states your wishes regarding medical treatment should you become unable to make or communicate those desires.

environmental cost associated with their use is exceptionally high. The design and improvements of our communities and rural areas center around accommodating cars rather than pedestrians and bicyclists—from interstate highways to parking lots to massive freeway structures that dominate cities. We have become so accustomed to cars as a way of life that we often cease to notice how pervasive they are and how dependent we have become. Many tasks can now be accomplished without ever leaving one's car—there are drive-up windows at restaurants, banks, convenience stores, liquor stores, dry cleaners, and express mail services. Some communities have mortuaries with drive-up display windows for viewing the body of the deceased and paying last respects!

Use of technology is a major factor in the workplace. Machines once dominated primarily factories and other blue-collar work sites, but now they are a significant part of the white-collar workplace, too. Photocopying machines use hazardous chemicals and produce harmful **ozone**. Fatigue and headaches may be associated with sitting under fluorescent lights for several hours. Computer screens produce low-level radiation that some health experts believe warrants concern. Word processors make many secretarial tasks easier but have resulted in new health problems—deterioration of vision and carpal tunnel syndrome, a painful inflammatory condition that develops from repetitive hand and wrist motions. Although using a word processor can reduce the time needed to accomplish a given task, employees

Ozone: A rare, poisonous form of oxygen; ozone occurs naturally in the upper atmosphere where it absorbs harmful ultraviolet radiation from the sun; ozone is a harmful air pollutant at ground level, where it forms as a byproduct of a variety of manufacturing processes and types of combustion.

(continued on p. 96)

Except for the lucky few who work at home or within walking distance of it, everybody who works must commute—and most do it by car. It's not your imagination that traffic has gotten worse lately, and it's no secret why. Corporate headquarters have spread into the suburbs and exurbs, so that many people find themselves driving from one burb to another, rather than going to the center of town by train or bus. The

When Rush Hour Never Ends

quest for affordable housing has in some cases pushed people farther from where they work and from existing public transportation. Adding to the clog is the two-paycheck family—each worker in a separate car. Most people actively dislike commuting. And a few drivers swing out of control.

[During 1987] on freeways in southern California, 70 drivers got angry enough (usually in afternoon or early evening traffic) to assault their fellow motorists with deadly weapons. This wasn't just West Coast craziness, as some East Coast newspapers claimed. Similar incidents had occurred earlier in Houston, St. Louis, and Detroit. Studies conducted in both England and Utah have revealed that a significant number of people agreed with the statement, "At times I could gladly kill another driver." At a [recent] UCLA symposium, Raymond Novaco of the University of California, Irvine, reported on a survey of 287 California college students. It showed that one out of 10 of them had become so angry in traffic that they hurled some object at another driver. Any driver knows that impatient horn-honking, shouted insults, and obscene gestures are nothing unusual on the highway. Is it safe to go to work by car? Can you keep from being infected by the madness?

Very few people commit violence, even with daily exposure to heavy traffic. As Novaco pointed out, the people arrested in the California shootings were not commuters driven berserk by traffic jams. One man brought to trial and convicted of manslaughter had a record of assaults and had been drinking heavily when he shot his victim. Nevertheless, in an earlier study Novaco found that "chronic exposure to traffic congestion" produces "an increase in baseline blood pressure, lowering of frustration tolerance, increases in negative mood, and aggressive driving habits." Your personality can play a role, too. If you tend to be impatient and aggressive, traffic may be harder for you to handle.

The quality of your commute is also important. Borrowing from the language of electric circuitry, transportation researchers have come up with the term *impedance,* meaning "restraints on movement and goal attainment." In one study commuters were assigned an "impedance rating." For example, a low-impedance driver might travel 7 miles in 12 minutes, while it might take a higher-impedance driver 30 minutes to cover the same 7 miles. High-impedance drivers were likelier to arrive home with higher blood pressure and in a worse mood than others. Stressful commuting impaired "personal well-being, job satisfaction, and quality of home life." Even easygoing personalities reacted adversely.

One cheerful note: commuters under heavy stress usually strive to improve the situation. In some areas it may be possible to switch to public transportation or a car pool. Perhaps you can stagger your work hours so that you need not travel at the height of the rush. Car radios and cassette players are excellent investments. Listening to educational tapes (or audio-books) may reduce tension and make the time pass profitably. Keep in mind that nothing—absolutely nothing—will be gained by responding angrily to the irate squawk of the horn to the rear of you, or the ugly gesture that you glimpse in passing. If your fellow motorist is clearly furious with you, check quickly to see if you're doing something reprehensible (crowding the next lane, not reacting to a green light). If so, try to do better. But remember that the driver shouting obscenities from the next car may have been drinking, and is certainly out of control. Ignore him and, as soon as possible, drive on.

Source: *University of California Berkeley Wellness Letter*, Vol. 4, No. 12, September 1988, pp. 1–2.

may be given and expected to produce more work during the day as a result. Facsimile (fax) machines, overnight delivery services, and car phones mean one can always be in touch with the rest of the world, but they also produce new expectations and pressures about work deadlines.

In the home, electric blankets seem innocuous enough, yet experts now recommend that pregnant women not sleep under them because of harmful effects on the fetus from low-level radiation. [13] In the physician's office, X rays help in the diagnosis of some diseases and conditions, yet unwarranted use needlessly exposes patients to harmful radiation.

Television affects the health of people at all ages; all but a very small percentage of homes own one or more televisions. How attached we are to these entertaining boxes is indicated by a recent poll in which nearly 40 percent of viewers admitted that they keep the television in their homes turned on even when not watching it. [14] Children view television, on the average, for close to 4 hours a day. By the time a child has reached the age of 20, he or she will have watched 150,000 commercials for toys, candy, sugared cereals, and other less-than-nutritious food products, over-the-counter medications, and numerous other consumer goods—and will have foregone thousands of hours of more active pursuits. Research indicates that obesity levels in teenagers increase by 2 percent for every hour of television watched daily. Men who watch television for at least 3 hours a day are twice as likely to be obese as those who watch less than one hour, even when exercise habits and other factors are considered. [15]

In many ways, technology and **consumerism** are intertwined. Advertisers appeal to our desire to accomplish tasks with less effort and encourage us to buy equipment that makes chores easier and reduces physical effort. Why push a lawn mower when you can ride one? Why cut vegetables by hand when you can use a slicer-dicer-mixer-chopper machine? And why take a walk in the evening when you can hop on an exercise machine, turn on the television, and view commercials about more new products? As the number of calories we burn through daily activity steadily decreases, we struggle to keep extra pounds from creeping on with the years. Finding the time to burn more calories becomes a goal. Those who can afford it can drive to a local health spa and jog on the latest treadmill with electronic pulse monitoring capability, pacing dials, and mileage readouts. Exercise equipment sales are booming. One could argue that machines both take away our health and give it back!

In making decisions about the use of various types of technology in your own life, keep in mind not just the specific benefit something provides, but its impact on your life as a whole. How does a new technology affect your fitness level? Does it expose you or others to harmful fumes, chemicals, or radiation? Does incorporating a given technology in your life mean that other, more beneficial pursuits and interests will suffer? Does production, use, or disposal of the technology adversely affect the environment? Machines and other forms of technology are so pervasive in our lives that they have a major impact on health. By considering technological advances in the context of this larger picture, we can make wiser decisions about their appropriate use.

ENVIRONMENTAL HEALTH

Deforestation in both tropical countries and in our own, **acid rain**, air pollution, ozone destruction, land contaminated with industrial chemicals, pesticides in the water supply, and widespread soil erosion from unsustainable agricultural practices—these are but a few of the serious environmental crises of today.

As biological organisms, we are completely dependent on the health of our environment. For example, as the destruction of the

Consumerism: The movement that seeks to protect the rights of consumers against fraud, overcharging, unsafe or unhealthful products, and other abuses or damage caused by dishonest or careless business practices.

Deforestation: The deliberate or inadvertent removal of trees from the land resulting in a reduction of forest area.

Acid rain: Rain that contains relatively high concentrations of acid-forming air pollutants such as sulfur and nitrogen oxides.

earth's protective ozone layer from industrial chemicals has progressed, rates of malignant skin cancer have risen sharply because of greater exposure to **ultraviolet rays**. Entire communities have experienced high rates of cancer and sickness from pollution of their environs with toxic chemicals by local industry. In 1972 the Environmental Protection Agency reported the majority of community water supplies they had tested contained dangerous residues of industrial contaminants, a situation still not under control. [16]

The environmental catastrophes we hear the most about—the toxic chemicals of Love Canal, the nuclear radiation of Chernobyl, the thousands of deaths caused by pesticide production in Bhopal, India, the Exxon oil spill in Alaska, and the oil spill in the Persian Gulf—are only the tip of the iceberg. Environmental problems are now present in every community and every country, whether the issue is landfill, air pollution, soil erosion, safe water, forest preservation, radiation exposure, or **global warming** and climatic changes.

Approaches to restoring the environment vary widely, from those of members of the organization "Earth First!" who have lain down in front of bulldozers to protest forest destruction, to the business-like approach of the Nature Conservancy, an organization that raises funds and simply buys land of environmental importance in order to preserve it. Many think we need stronger laws punishing industrial polluters, stricter regulations regarding auto emissions, industrial and agricultural chemicals, and other sources of pollution, and much stronger enforcement of laws already in place.

While haphazard and careless practices by industry contribute a major blow to the health of land, air, and water, individual habits play a role as well. Our growth-dependent economy has created a consumer mentality that many think has exceeded healthy bounds—we are often called the "throw-away" society. Our landfills overflow with packaging from our grocery and fast-food purchases, for example, and we are accustomed to buying the latest model of the latest technology—whether it is a car, stereo, videocassette recorder, or television—and throwing out the old. We use vast quantities of plastic and paper products, disposable diapers, and styrofoam. Such consumer goods use up natural resources, require industrial chemicals and significant water use in their production, and wind up in landfill dumps, where their component chemicals leach into the ground and water supply.

There are relatively simple steps individuals can take to reduce the impact on the environment from daily living, such as

Ultraviolet rays: Light rays whose wavelength is less than that of the shortest visible light yet longer than that of X rays; prolonged exposure to ultraviolet light is potentially harmful.

Global warming: A gradual increase in the average annual temperature of the earth that some experts believe is currently underway and has the potential to cause many harmful effects.

FIGURE 5.4
Percentage Breakdown of Garbage in the United States

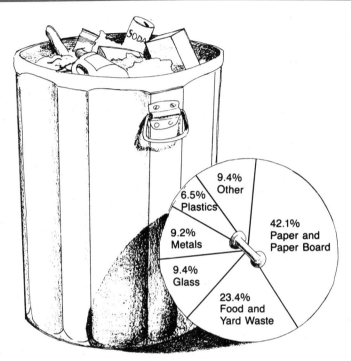

Source: Environmental Protection Agency.

The average American generates 3.5 pounds of trash a day. Paper and paper products account for over 40 percent of this total.

Did You Know That . . .

Contrary to popular opinion, newspapers do not biodegrade completely. Recent archaeological digs in several garbage dumps revealed legible copies that had been buried for 40 years.

recycling cans, newspapers, glass, cardboard, and plastic; not buying products that come in excessive packaging; avoiding use of pesticides and toxic chemicals at home that enter the sewer and ground; riding a bicycle or walking rather than driving; and generally learning to be a little more content with fewer goods.

Such individual changes can be an important first step in learning about one's impact on the environment and the environmental health of one's community, country, and planet. Becoming active in legislative efforts or issues of local and national environmental groups is another worthwhile step. Coping with our current environmental crisis will take thoughtful policy development and strong enforcement, communities of people who are
(continued on p. 101)

Things You Can Do to Help the Environment

RECYCLE, REDUCE WASTE, BUY WISELY

- Buy only what you need.
- Buy products in bulk or with as little packaging as possible.
- Buy stationery and computer paper made from recycled paper.
- Buy things of wood, glass, or paper rather than plastic or styrofoam.
- Buy beverages in returnable bottles.
- Don't buy aerosol cans (CFCs destroy the ozone).
- Use phosphate-free, biodegradable soaps and detergents and non-toxic cleaning products.
- Use plates, mugs, cloth napkins, and dish towels instead of paper plates, cups, napkins, and towels.
- Use cloth diapers for infants rather than disposables.
- Avoid fast food restaurants, with their excessive use of styrofoam, plastic, and paper packaging.
- Recycle motor oil, glass bottles, cans, cardboard, office paper, plastic, and newspaper.
- Don't buy tropical wood, unless you are sure it is from a sustainable tree farm.
- Buy locally grown produce grown without pesticides and chemical fertilizers.
- Buy at local farmers' markets.

IN THE HOME

- Have an energy audit of your home done; insulate windows, walls, attic, and water heater.
- Turn down the thermostat in winter and put on a sweater.
- Limit use of air-conditioning in home and car.
- Install water-saving shower heads, faucets, and toilet devices.

- Don't let unneeded water run while brushing teeth, or washing dishes and clothes.
- Grow a vegetable garden rather than a lawn to reduce water waste.
- Eat lower on the food chain (more grains, fruit, and vegetables; less meat).
- Hand-wash rather than have clothes dry-cleaned (dry-cleaning solvents destroy the ozone).

ON THE MOVE

- Car pool to work, walk, or ride a bike.
- Use buses and other public transportation.
- Drive a fuel-efficient car.

GET INVOLVED

- Join local environmental and neighborhood groups working on issues that affect your community.
- Lobby your city to start programs in curbside, oil, and CFC (from old refrigerators and air-conditioners) recycling.
- Pressure fast food chains to reduce use of packaging.
- Write congressmen and senators in support of timber practice reform on public lands and saving of old-growth forests.
- Support and write governmental leaders regarding agriculture reforms that encourage sustainable growing methods, small farms, organic farming practices.
- Lobby governmental leaders in support of building light rail lines, improving bus or other transportation lines in your vicinity.
- Write letters to your local newspapers on issues you are concerned about.

willing to address and speak out about concerns, and cooperation between countries on critical issues—as well as changes in personal life-style.

A healthy environment may also depend on approaches and attitudes that promote long-term solutions rather than short-term economic gains that last for a generation or less. Early Native Americans often expressed the need to consider the impact of their decisions on future generations.

Promoting one's personal health through a positive life-style is an irreplaceable factor in well-being, but attending to the health of the environment that provides the soil our food is grown in, the water we drink, the air we breathe, and the species, forests, and **ecosystems** essential to a healthy planet is of equal importance—and deserving of some of the energy we put toward living well. W

Ecosystem: A dynamic community that comprises all of the living creatures and their total environment within a specified area.

CHAPTER

6

Taking Charge

TO PROMOTE HEALTH we need not only an increase in knowledge but an ability to initiate and maintain changes in behaviors based on new knowledge. Our level of wellness is determined by our living habits and the hundreds of small choices and decisions we make every day. After taking the "Healthstyle" self-test at the end of chapter 2, you now have a sense of the life-style changes that will be the most beneficial for you to make. You probably had an idea of this already—most people are aware of at least some of the positive behaviors they would like to incorporate permanently into their lives. For one reason or another, however, many of us don't experience long-term success in maintaining these changes. We have all attempted an improvement in our life-styles at one time or another—whether we were trying to lose weight, get more exercise, eat better, and so forth—but return to the comfortable old patterns within a few weeks.

There is an art to implementing and maintaining change. Learning specific techniques makes the difference between experiencing the satisfaction of achieving your goal and frustration and self-blame for falling short. By applying the following behavior-change steps, you will have an excellent chance of maintaining your new, healthy life-style patterns:

Determine What You Want to Change Choose only one specific behavior, habit, or life-style area. Do you want to become more fit, lower your cholesterol, manage stress better, drink less, or develop more friendships and leisure time activities? Don't attempt to make too many changes at once. You are most likely to

(continued on p. 105)

Remaking Our Lives

Your frumpy cousin shows up at Christmas 30 lb. lighter and looking great—and you finally decide it's time to start getting in shape. You find yourself driving through a blizzard to buy cigarettes, and suddenly turn around, swearing to kick the habit. Maybe your spouse finally persuades you to drink a little less—or your boss finally pushes you too far, and you quit. Whatever your personal story, you've almost certainly experienced the sudden revelation that makes you see things in a new way, and leads you to change your life.

But despite its universality, we still know remarkably little about the hows and whys of change. What gets us going? How many of us go back to our old ways? Are quitting smoking and drinking as hard as we think? Most crucial of all, what gives a person a new sense of self?

To find the answers, *American Health* and the Campbell Soup Company cosponsored an exclusive Gallup survey. More than a thousand Americans provided surprising new information about the dynamics of change:

■ **Positive feelings, not fear or self-disgust, motivate most people to change.**
■ **People are about 10 times likelier to change on their own than to be helped by doctors, therapists or self-help groups.**
■ **A sudden insight or unpredictable event is likelier to push someone into action than a carefully developed plan.**
■ **People are powerfully motivated by concern for their health to exercise, change their diets and lose weight.**
■ **Quitting smoking and drinking are actually *easier* than other kinds of change for many people.**

Taken together, the survey's findings demonstrate the ability we all have to transform our lives. Whether you're trying to find a new job or kick a bad habit, the new evidence shows you can do it—and probably without intricate strategies or expensive help.

Men and women are equally open to change. But in general, those who are young and well educated tend to welcome change the most. (Generally, people make more important life changes during their 20s than at any other time.)

When we gave each person we interviewed a list of 11 different kinds of life changes, we found that 90% had made at least one. We then asked each person to tell us which had been the two or three *most important* changes in his or her life, and asked follow-up questions only about those crucial transformations. Here's what we found.

JUST DO IT!

When it comes to changing your life, spontaneity is the rule. Our respondents said there was no special event that pushed them to change—they just *did* it—51% of the time. When there was a specific trigger for change, unpredictable turns of events, like hitting a physical or emotional crisis, were more likely to spur people into action than making a New Year's resolution or passing a significant birthday (each cited less than 1% of the time). Change usually doesn't start with a complicated strategy, either; for three-quarters of the changes people made, they began "day by day, without any particular plan."

Professional help has surprisingly little to do with important life changes, even health-related ones. Doctors helped people change only 3% of the time—while psychologists and psychiatrists, self-help groups and religious counselors got the credit even less often. Support was much more likely to come from friends (14%), parents, children or siblings (21%), or a spouse, boyfriend or girlfriend(29%). And 30% of the time, people simply did what they had to do on their own, often with striking success.

THE ADDICTIONS: ALCOHOL AND TOBACCO

In a major surprise, we learned that a full 70% of those who cut down on alcohol and 54% of those who quit smoking said, "It was easy to change—I just decided to do it one day." Most quit on their own, too, saying help from others "really didn't make a difference one way or the other."

It's possible, of course, that people with severe addictions have a harder time of it. But for most people, giving up smoking or excessive drinking seems to be not only relatively easy, but permanent.

A majority of people who made other lifestyle changes said they had slipped and gone back to their old ways at least once or twice. In contrast, 55% of those who'd cut back their drinking—and a stunning 72% of ex-smokers—said they had *never* relapsed. Ex-smokers have a particularly long track record: More than half quit over five years ago.

STRESS, EMOTIONS AND RELATIONSHIPS

Emotional changes, such as overcoming depression or a phobia, are the hardest to make. Half of those who overcame emotional problems or changed their relationships said, "It was difficult—it took a fair amount of thought and effort." Roughly a third said, "It was the hardest thing I've ever done."

Nevertheless, it's worth the trouble. Making a difficult inner change has a positive ripple effect—even more so than diet or exercise changes. More than two-thirds of those who overcame emotional problems (68%) reported, "Once I changed this aspect of my life, I wanted to change other aspects, too." Interestingly, stress-reduction programs were even more powerful agents of change: 85% of those who learned to control stress found they then wanted to improve their lives in other ways.

DIET, WEIGHT AND EXERCISE

These health-related changes may take more vigilance than giving up alcohol and tobacco. Even so, about half of those who had taken up exercise or started eating a healthier diet said it was "easy"—and most said they needed little outside help.

When it comes to weight loss, 35% of us

reduce for our health, 35% to look better, and 27% to feel better physically. But for exercise—despite all the spandex outfits in designer colors—health is *twice* as likely as appearance to be the main motivator. Health is also the overwhelming reason people change their diets nutritionally or quit smoking—and it's a special concern for older people, who are most likely to make those two changes.

WORK AND PLAY

The commonest life change is starting a new hobby. The shift cited most often as "important" is changing your career. But whether you're focused on work or play, the goal may be to make life more interesting. While 32% of those who made a career change did it to make more money, 18% changed for the intellectual stimulation, and 10% to feel better emotionally. A leading reason people became involved in social causes, too, was to do something interesting with their lives.

POWER OF POSITIVE FEELINGS

Regardless of what kind of change was at issue, we found encouraging news: People are able to maintain new lifestyles for long periods, and it gets easier as they go along. On average, our interview subjects made their important changes between one and five years ago, and hadn't slipped back to their old ways.

Fully 86% of the time, the people we interviewed agreed that "as time goes on, my new habits have become easy to keep up—they make me feel good." Most didn't have to reward themselves for being "good" (say, buying a new dress for every 10 lb. lost), or scare themselves about the consequences of a relapse (gaining those 10 lb. back).

Despite the cliché of the alcoholic who goes on the wagon after a bender, only 14% of changes happened because someone had "hit bottom." More often, people changed because they already felt good about themselves and wanted to feel even better—not because they were angry at themselves.

PUSHING BEYOND COMFORT

Although the odds of success are good, change is never easy. As a 36-year-old man who changed his career put it, the biggest difficulty is "stepping beyond the comfort zone." That defines in a nutshell the process of change. We form habits because they serve the purpose of comforting us, for a time—say, smoking or drinking to allay our anxiety, or staying in an old, unhappy relationship because it's reassuringly familiar.

To change, we have to be willing to give up the comforts we've outgrown for something better; autonomy, health, true happiness. It's a risk we each take alone. But this survey shows that if you make that leap of faith, you're likely to land on your feet.

—*Joel Gurin*

Which Changes Have You Made?

Took up a new *hobby,* sport or other "fun" activity	46%
Started an *exercise* program	45%
Made a major change in *diet*	41%
Overcame an *emotional problem,* like depression, anxiety, phobias or shyness	40%
Decided to change a major *relationship* with my spouse, parents or someone else in an important way	37%
Chose to make a major *career* change	37%
Became active in a *social cause,* such as the environment or helping the homeless	32%
Cut way down on *alcohol*	31%
Lost a significant amount of *weight*	25%
Stopped *smoking*	24%
Started a *stress-relief program,* such as meditation, a new religious practice or a new philosophical approach	20%

(Adds up to more than 100% because respondents could choose more than one answer. Results are from 1,026 adults interviewed by telephone in October 1989. Sampling error is plus or minus 3%.)

Source: Joel Gurin, *American Health* (March 1990), pp. 50–52.

succeed if you work on one area at a time. If you ultimately want to make more than one improvement, let the other areas wait until you have accomplished the first change and experienced the satisfaction of success. By then you will have developed even more confidence and motivation for making the next change.

Determine Where You Are and Where You Are Going Collect "baseline data" on yourself: What are your current behaviors in the area you have chosen to change? Once you have determined where you are now, determine where you want to be.

For example, Mary notes that she has tension headaches several times a week; she also feels she is under considerable stress. For several days she pays attention to the times at which she feels her shoulder and neck muscles tightening and the situations that trigger the tension. She decides to develop stress management and relaxation skills to reduce both her stress and symptoms of stress when she anticipates these trigger situations will be occurring.

As another example, John thinks he may be drinking too much but is not really sure. He conscientiously notes how many beers he consumes over the course of two weeks, sees it is a bit more than he thought, and determines a reasonable limit for himself.

Many of us have distorted notions of the level of our current behaviors. Before you plan a change, you need to know very clearly where you are starting from so that you can plan reasonable changes. Take the time to observe yourself closely. Tools for this include a food record, stress diary, physical activity log, or another means of recording behavior.

Assess Your Motivation   Sit down and carefully think through all of your reasons for wanting to make a change. In your mind, complete the statement, "I want to make this change because . . ." What are the benefits to you? Include benefits related to physical health, mental health, stress, energy level, and appearance—whatever is relevant to you. Some people find it helpful to write these down. Be sure that you are making this change because you want to, not because of outside pressure from other people.

Now, look at your list, assess your motivation and commitment level, and decide—are you really ready? Are the benefits great enough in your mind that you feel you are motivated and committed to make the change? If not, realize that you can choose a different goal or a smaller goal. You can even choose to make your change in the future, when you may be more motivated.

Make Your Goal Specific   State your goal in precise terms, being as specific as possible about what you will accomplish. "I want to become more fit" is a worthy goal, but it is not specific enough for you to see clearly what you must do to get there. A more well-defined goal is needed, such as, "I will jog regularly for the next three months." Be realistic in setting goals such as distance—don't plan to start off jogging 5 miles a day if you haven't jogged around the block recently.

Setting a very specific goal for yourself is the most important part of behavior change, and its value cannot be overemphasized. "I am going to drink less" is less likely to get you where you want to be than "I will limit myself to 2 alcoholic drinks per evening and drink 5 days per week only." People seldom accomplish successful change if they do not have a clear vision of where they are now, where they are going, and how they will get there.

FIGURE 6.1
Exercise

Joining a sports team at work, school, or in your community is an excellent way to get regular exercise.

Make An Action Plan   You now need to take your goal and state it in even more specific, measurable, and accomplishable terms. Vague, general statements or thoughts about making an improvement don't guide us well and only create discomfort and dissatisfaction when they hang over us like a cloud of judgment. For example, if you have decided to become more fit by engaging in a regular jogging program, you now need to determine the "when, where, and how long" of your goal. You might decide you will start by jogging:

• at a slow pace for 20 minutes
• around the neighborhood
• after work or class in the late afternoon
• every other day, beginning this Sunday
• for the next 6 weeks.

Table 6.1 The Most Popular Ways to Lose Weight

Just cut out snacks and desserts	42%
Just eat less of everything	37%
Start to exercise more	32%
Cut down on fat	32%
Stop eating at night	29%
Eat more fruits and vegetables	20%
Start counting calories	19%
Eat less red meat	17%
Use low-calorie foods and drinks	12%
Follow a diet plan from a doctor	11%
Eat more filling, low-calorie foods	10%
Join a weight-loss group	9%
Use a special diet food (e.g., protein powder)	3%
Follow a diet book	1%

Source: Joel Gurin, "Eating Goes Back to Basics," *American Health* (March 1990), p. 98.

Here are the ways in which people who responded to a recent survey indicated they had successfully lost weight.

You now have a clear vision of what you will need to do and when you will need to do it in order to accomplish your primary goal of becoming more fit. Without such a road map, it is far too easy to see your good intentions slip away along with busy days, intervening activities, and the lapses in motivation we all experience.

Assess Your Plan Now you must apply some realism and pragmatism to your plan. Can you really accomplish what you have said you will do?

If you can determine that you have at least an 80 percent chance of accomplishing your goal as you have specifically stated it, then you are in good shape. If that is not the case, then make adjustments. Decide to engage in the new behavior less often, to a lesser degree, or to scale the behavior down or change it in some way so it can be accomplished. Consider your current habits and preferences, your time schedule, and your environment. Don't set yourself up for failure, but for success. Be realistic with yourself.

The most frequent reason why people fail in their changes is that they attempt to do too much, too quickly. They decide to

Table 6.2 The Biggest Dietary Changes

Eat less fat	46%
Eat more fruits and vegetables	44%
Cut down on candy, sweets and desserts	40%
Eat less cholesterol	35%
Cut down on salt and salty snacks	32%
Eat less red meat	31%
Eat more chicken and fish	22%
Cut down on coffee, caffeinated sodas	13%
Eat more "health foods"	9%
Take more vitamins	7%

Source: Joel Gurin, "Eating Goes Back to Basics," *American Health* (March 1990), p. 98.

Here are the most important dietary changes undertaken by the people who responded to the survey mentioned in table 6.1.

become more fit and so attempt to run 5 miles a day by the end of their first week, work too hard at exercise, develop severe muscle soreness, lose any sense of pleasure from what should be a joyful process, and quickly give up, deciding that exercise is simply too painful, too difficult, and too time-consuming. Or they determine they eat too much fat and attempt to go "cold turkey" on foods they have been eating and enjoying for years.

To be successful, you may need to pull back on the reins a bit, start small, be patient, and be proud of accomplishing smaller steps that take you to your larger goal.

Analyze Obstacles Even the best laid plans can go astray. Think through carefully or make a list of the barriers and obstacles likely to keep you from carrying out your plan. For example, resolving to change certain eating patterns is difficult if you are often in social situations where foods you are trying to avoid are offered. A means of dealing with this potential pitfall needs to be developed. It may be as simple as affirming to yourself ahead of time that you will say "no, thank you" or making a deal with yourself to splurge a little and enjoy one thing but not eat the cake, the pie, *and* the ice cream. Be flexible and develop realistic ways to deal with situations.

As another example, some common barriers to exercise that people cite are lack of time, fear of harassment while out exercising, less than optimal weather, not having comfortable shoes, and lack of knowledge, which may cause a person experiencing some initial muscle soreness to give up. Each of these barriers can be dealt with if they are thought through ahead of time.

For example, to deal with lack of time, you may need to allow for exercise on your calendar and give it the same priority as a doctor's appointment. Or you may need to get up a half hour earlier in the morning. Family cooperation or child-care arrangements may be needed if time away from children is required. Talking to a physical education teacher or a friend who exercises or buying a book on exercise can solve the lack-of-knowledge barrier. Make contingency plans to get around weather conditions. You can, for example, decide to have an indoor workout with a video or a stationary bicycle instead of an outdoor workout. The point is to think through the obstacles you are likely to face and determine ahead of time how you will remain flexible yet overcome the barrier so that you remain fairly on track with your plan. Small deviations from your plan are not cause for giving up or thinking you are a failure. They are inevitable, in fact, and the successful person is one who understands this reality and determines to remain committed to the new life-style pattern in spite of the ups and downs that may occur along the road.

Measure Your Success and Reward Yourself Because you have stated your goal in specific terms, it should be easy to keep track of how you are doing. You should be able to tell on a daily or weekly basis if you are following your plan. If not, now is the time to make adjustments, analyze barriers again, and plan things a little differently to optimize your chances of success. Here again, keeping records can be helpful in observing your progress.

Similarly, take the time to feel pleased with yourself for the changes you have made, whether or not they are as large as you had hoped. Very small steps can be just as important as the bigger steps. Share your accomplishments with an interested and supportive friend—you deserve a pat on the back, and you can also serve as a source of inspiration to others attempting change. If it is helpful, give yourself a reward for your efforts. After meeting a goal, or after incorporating a change into their lives for several weeks, many people find it helps them stay with the change if they periodically reward themselves with something special—a movie, new clothes, a weekend trip, a new book, or something else to which they would not normally treat themselves. The reward can be determined in advance as part of your action plan, too, as a "carrot" to keep you on track.

Keep Adding Reinforcement As time goes by, the newness and challenge of incorporating new habits can wear off, and it becomes important to build sources of continued support into your life. For example, participating in community fun runs, beginning to run competitively, or joining a health spa, a community or work-site sports team, or a fitness class are ways of adding a new and pleasurable dimension to exercise. Joining an interest club or a self-help group can be useful, as can reading books; subscribing to health, fitness, or hobby magazines; taking classes and workshops; and spending time with others who are involved and interested in the same areas. Family members may become interested in the activity, making it more likely you will maintain your changes. Keep learning, talking to others, trying new approaches, and assessing how you are doing. Periodically think back to where you were a month ago, six months, a year—you may be surprised and pleased to realize how far you have come.

Use the Action Plan at the end of this chapter to plan your chosen life-style improvement.

BEING A WISE HEALTH CONSUMER

We all become ill or injured at times and need professional medical assistance. To ensure that this assistance is as beneficial as possible, one needs to take an active part in the decisions and treatment process. Involvement in medical care decisions, following medical advice, and addressing preventive health-care needs through appropriate medical tests and exams are crucial to maintaining lifelong wellness. One basic preventive measure that everyone should take is to ensure that his or her **immunizations** are current. See the box entitled "Wrap Up: Immunization" on the following page.

Periodic Health Screenings
Although many health experts, physicians among them, think the value of the annual physical exam is overrated, there are certain exams and tests that you should have done periodically. The specific tests needed and how often they are needed vary according to age, sex, and medical condition. For example, both children and adults need up-to-date immunizations, but the specific immunizations needed are different. Adults should have their cholesterol and blood pressure checked at regular intervals, along with several other tests. Women need regular **Pap smears**. At certain times of life, specific tests will be needed that are not needed at other times. If you think you have been exposed to a

(continued on p. 113)

Did You Know That . . .

Seeing and feeling the positive results of maintaining a healthier life-style can reinforce efforts toward better health. These include better muscle tone, less body fat, improved breathing and fewer colds after quitting smoking, compliments from others, and a general sense of renewed energy.

Immunization: The process of artificially bolstering the body's immunity against certain infectious diseases by the administration of a vaccine or other type of medication.

Pap smear: A test designed to detect abnormal changes in a small sample containing cells from the surface of the cervix (the neck of the uterus) thus preventing cervical cancer.

Wrap-up: Immunization

In this century immunization with vaccines has had more of an impact on contagious diseases than all of the other health services available to us. Smallpox, once the most widespread disease in the world, has been virtually eradicated everywhere. And in the U.S. and other developed countries, diseases such as diphtheria, tetanus, polio, and whooping cough—which 50 years ago were killing or crippling hundreds of thousands of people—have largely been brought under control.

Yet as long as even a few cases of a disease occur within a population, people who are not immunized are at risk of catching it. Moreover, when immunization coverage drops, diseases can return with a vengeance, as has happened with whooping cough. That is why [experts have endorsed] at least three major immunization campaigns: for children entering school; for college-age adults at risk of getting measles or rubella; and for older adults at risk of getting influenza and its complications.

How does immunization work? It prevents diseases caused by microbes—bacteria and viruses—that for the most part cannot be effectively treated. The body builds immunity naturally when it catches a disease and responds by forming antibodies, which kill the invading microbes or render them harmless. Vaccines create immunity artificially—and more safely—because they contain modified microbes or toxins that aren't strong enough to cause disease, yet can still stimulate our systems to produce antibodies. Once a person is vaccinated with a particular microbe, he will fend off a subsequent infection by the same microbe with an immediate outpouring of antibodies.

American children are supposed to be routinely immunized against the leading contagious diseases—and they are. According to recent estimates, 90% of preschoolers have now been immunized. However, this makes many adults complacent about immunization, which is dangerous because they need to maintain certain types of immunity. For example, even if you were immunized against tetanus and diphtheria as a child, you need to receive booster shots periodically to remain fully protected. Yet nearly half of American adults are not up to date on their boosters.

Some 40 million adults should get a flu vaccine each fall. Outbreaks of influenza occur virtually every year, usually in winter, and can cause thousands of people to be hospitalized. But only about 20% of the people who should be receiving flu shots are getting them. The same figures apply to a new vaccine for bacterial pneumonia. Also, adults in certain occupational and life-style groups, such as college students and health-care workers, may be at high risk and should be immunized.

Along with being complacent, many adults are skeptical about the effectiveness and safety of the vaccines intended to protect them. For example, influenza vaccine, although advocated by health officials, has never been widely accepted by the public. Resistance to it was especially strong after the winter of 1976–77, when a vaccine for combating swine flu was associated with about 500 cases of a rare paralytic condition called Guillain-Barré syndrome. Because of the wide publicity this received, the safety of flu vaccine was seriously challenged—even though nearly 48 million people got vaccinations that winter without serious consequences. What is most reassuring is that the influenza vaccines used since have *not* been associated with Guillain-Barré syndrome or other substantial side effects. Yet a majority of the people who could benefit from flu vaccine ignore it.

Based on a wide number of studies, however, modern vaccines have been judged to be extremely safe and effective by the American Academy of Pediatrics, the American College of Physicians, and the Centers for Disease Control in Atlanta. This does not mean that adverse effects from vaccines have been eliminated. But the chances of a severe reaction occurring in a healthy adult are extremely slim. For most individuals, as well as for the society at large, there is no doubt that the benefits of immunization far outweigh the risks.

Source: *University of California Berkeley Wellness Letter,* Vol. 1, No. 12, September 1985, p. 4.

sexually transmitted disease, for example, you shouldn't wait for symptoms to appear before you get tested.

Some exams that are needed regularly you can perform yourself, such as monthly breast self-exams in women and testicular self-exams in men. Other tests need to be performed at a health clinic or a physician's office.

The tests needed by males and females at different ages are shown in figure 6.4.

Health Promotion Tests and Screenings

In addition to standard preventive health tests, such as blood pressure and cholesterol checks, other kinds of assessments can be useful. Most communities, student health centers, or employee wellness programs may offer one or more of the following (some of these are also available from health clinics and physician's offices):

- Fitness assessment (for cardiorespiratory fitness, muscle strength/endurance, and flexibility)
- Skin cancer exam
- **Blood lipid profile** (cholesterol and other blood fats)

Blood lipid profile: A blood test administered to check the level of cholesterol and other fats in the blood.

FIGURE 6.2
Breast Self-Examination

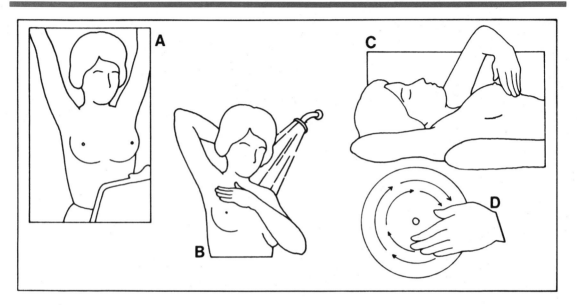

Source: Courtesty of the American Cancer Society.

It is important for a woman to examine her breasts regularly. She should look at her breasts in the mirror, first with her arms at her sides, then with them raised over her head (A). Visible warning signals include thickening, swelling, dimpling, skin irritation, distortion, retraction, or scaliness. In the shower, her hands can easily move over the wet skin (B). When she is lying down a woman can easily examine her breast tissue as it is distributed (C). The fingers should be held flat and move in complete clockwise circles around the outer portion of the breast then move progressively inward toward the nipple (D). Warning signals that can be detected include a lump or lumps, thickening, pain or tenderness of the nipple, or discharge.

- Diabetes test
- Body fat or body composition analysis
- Vision exam
- Hearing test
- Back health exam
- Computerized Health Risk Appraisal
- Computerized or self-scored life stress assessment
- Computerized nutrition/diet assessment

If you see these services offered in your community, take advantage of them. Save your results in a personal "wellness file" so you can refer to them when you are tested again in the future.

FIGURE 6.3
Testicular Self-Examination

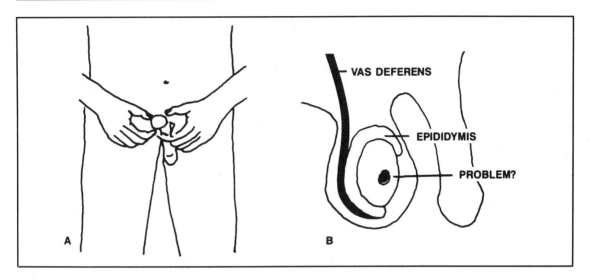

Source: Courtesy of the American Cancer Society.

The best time for a man to examine his testes is right after a hot bath or shower because the testicle descends and the scrotal skin relaxes in the heat. He should place his index and middle fingers on the underside of the testicle and his thumbs on top (A). He should gently roll the testicle between his fingers and thumb. Any abnormal lump is most likely to be found at the front or side of the testicle (B).

LIVING WELL

You have all the tools you need to develop a positive wellness lifestyle. This, more than any other factor, can give you energetic, healthy years and minimize your chances of developing the most common degenerative diseases of our time.

Remember that wellness is not a static state, but a process, and one in which you will keep changing, growing, and finding new ways to optimize your well-being. As you make changes and find new challenges for yourself, you will also be helping to pave the road for others to make positive changes. By paying attention to your own wellness and supporting others in their efforts, you can contribute to the health of your community and environment as well—both critical needs as we move into the '90s.

FIGURE 6.4
Recommended Health Exams

Examination	Birth–5	5–15	15–20	20–30	30–35	35–40	40–50	50–Over
Immunizations	Check With Your Doctor							
Blood Pressure		Every Year						
Cholesterol			Every 5 Years					
Pelvic Exam (Women)				Every 1–3 Years			Every Year	
Pap Smear (Women)				Following 2 Negative Annual Tests, Every 1–3 Years			Every Year	
Professional Breast Exam (Women)				Every 1–3 Years			Every Year	
Mammography (Women)						1 Baseline X-ray	Every 1–2 Years	Every Year
Blood Glucose			Every 3–5 Years					
Rectal Exam					Every 5 Years		Every Year	
Sigmoidoscopy (Colon-Rectal Cancer Screening)							Every 3–5 Years	
Electrocardiogram							One Baseline Test	

The periodic health evaluations listed above are important for the early detection and treatment of common diseases. Even if you don't undergo a complete physical exam annually, you should make sure the above tests are conducted. If any problems are detected, your physician will probably want to recheck you at shorter intervals than those shown here.

We will end our discussion of wellness with some wisdom from an 85-year-old woman:

"If I had my life to live over, I would start barefoot earlier in the spring and stay that way later in the fall. I would go to more dances. I would ride more merry-go-rounds. I would pick more daisies." [1]

(continued on p. 120)

Whether for the purpose of a routine checkup or for diagnosis and treatment of a health problem, you should feel comfortable and able to communicate well with your doctor. Your medical care will be most effective if you have confidence in your doctor's abilities, are comfortable with the manner in which the office is run, and are a partner in any medical decisions.

How to Choose a Doctor

You can find a doctor by asking for referrals from relatives, friends, nurses, or other health professionals. You can also call the local medical society or hospital. Family or general practitioners, pediatricians, specialists in internal medicine, and obstetricians/gynecologists most often provide long-term medical care. Specialists, such as cardiologists (heart specialists), oncologists (cancer specialists), and many others, are seen for specific problems. Before selecting a primary doctor or a specialist, find out if he or she is board certified in his or her specialty area. This means he or she has met rigorous training criteria established by a national medical organization. Also check to see if he or she is on the staff at one or more local hospitals, so you can be admitted to the hospital should the need arise.

Other factors to consider in choosing a doctor include whether appointments can be scheduled within a reasonable period of time, whether the doctor is available for phone calls, and whether there is after-hours backup in case of an urgent problem. Ask about basic fees and compare them to fees of other doctors in the area. At your appointment, note how long, if at all, the doctor kept you waiting after your appointment time and whether he or she rushed you or was relaxed, listened, and answered questions to your satisfaction. Was a careful exam given? Were findings, lab tests, medications, and treatment alternatives discussed? Were side effects of drugs and potential interactions with other medications or foods discussed? A competent doctor will acknowledge when a clear diagnosis of a problem cannot be made, will refer you to a specialist if necessary, and will encourage you to seek a second opinion from another doctor before a decision to have surgery is made.

You can make the most of your visit to the doctor if you come prepared—using written notes if necessary. Be prepared to name any medications you are taking and any problems or symptoms you are currently experiencing—their severity, how long you have been experiencing them, what brings them on, and the nature of the pain or discomfort.

If you are not satisfied with the care or treatment you are receiving, you have every right to voice your concerns verbally or in writing to the physician. If your concerns are not addressed to your satisfaction, find a physician with whom you are more comfortable. [2]

Western or **allopathic medical care** is the accepted mode of medical treatment in the United States and is especially effective in dealing with infectious disease and acute conditions or trauma. Many critics of allopathic medicine point out that chronic diseases and ongoing ailments are not well treated by the allopathic approach, which is often limited to alleviating symptoms without providing a lasting cure. Alternative medical modes have increasingly become available in the United States.

Alternative Health Care

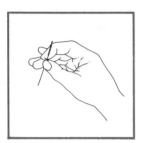

Acupuncture dates back to 2500 B.C. and is an ancient method of healing in China, where it is still used extensively to relieve pain and to cure diseases. Acupuncture involves inserting needles into the body at specific points. The healing ability of acupuncture is explained by the Chinese principle of *chi*, the body's vital energy current. The balance of two forces of *chi*, Yin and Yang, is said to determine the body's state of health. By inserting the needles at appropriate energy points along the body, these two forces can be brought back into balance and health restored. In the United States, some medical doctors have been trained in acupuncture and use it as an adjunct to their allopathic practice, most often for pain relief. Because acupuncture is considered an experimental medical procedure, some states limit its practice to licensed medical practitioners. Other states license nonphysician acupuncturists who have completed certain training requirements and passed an exam.

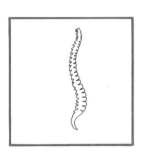

Chiropractic involves manipulation of the spine and is based on the tenet that disease is caused by vertebral misalignment. Many chiropractors also use nutrition, application of heat and cold, and herbal medicine as treatment. Spinal manipulation can clearly relieve the pain of musculoskeletal ailments, such as a stiff neck or wrenched back. Its value in treating disease is controversial. The chiropractic profession has been criticized for making patients go through prolonged regimens of treatment at excessive cost and for over-using spinal X rays, needlessly exposing patients to unnecessary radiation. Many patients report satisfactory treatment of symptoms that they were unable to get from their allopathic physicians, however. Doctors of Chiropractic (D.C.) receive their degrees from chiropractic schools.

Herbal medicine relies on treatment with the plant materials used for healing in cultures worldwide for thousands of years. Chinese physicians, Native American healers, and Hispanic curanderos make extensive use of herbal medicine. Many important drugs used today are derived from plants (such as digitalis from foxglove, quinine from the bark of a tree, ephedrine from the herb of the same name, etc.). Plants contain a wide range of pharmacologically active substances, both useful and toxic, and misuse of herbal medicine is potentially harmful. Andrew Weil, M.D., a physician and author who uses both allopathic and herbal pharmaceuticals, has pointed out that herbs are less likely to produce serious side effects than when their active compounds are isolated and concentrated for use in prescription medication, but herbal treatment requires knowledge, care, and monitoring.

Homeopathy is widely used in Europe and is undergoing a revival in the United States as well. One-third of French physicians use homeopathic remedies, and homeopathy is common in England and the Soviet Union. Homeopathy is based on the philosophy that small doses of a substance can stimulate the body's innate defenses and healing ability. Homeopathic remedies supply a very small amount of a substance in order to produce symptoms similar to the disease or illness, under the assumption that the body can slowly learn to deal with the malady and cure itself. Three states issue licenses for homeopaths (Nevada, Arizona, and Connecticut), but in reality, anyone can practice this form of treatment. Nonprescription homeopathic medicines are sold by mail, in health food stores, and in drugstores. They are exempt from Food and Drug Administration quality control regulations by virtue of a loophole in regulations. Scientific proof that the treatment mode works in some manner other than through eliciting a placebo effect has yet to surface. The only published studies indicating homeopathy's effectiveness proved controversial when close examination of the testing conditions indicated many errors in the method had occurred. Hopefully, further research will shed light on homeopathy.

Massage comes in many forms these days, from the most common Swedish massage to acupressure and connective tissue massage. Massage can help treat sore or tense muscles, improve circulation to injured body parts, and bring relief of pain. As a calming relaxation technique it is highly effective. Licensed Massage Therapists have received a degree from a certified massage school and completed many hours of hands-on practice.

Osteopathic medicine involves manipulation of the spine and is considered useful for musculoskeletal problems. Doctors of Osteopathy may also treat other illnesses and often place importance on nutritional habits. In the United States, Doctors of Osteopathy have the same medical privileges as medical doctors, such as access to hospital care for patients. Osteopathic physicians go through training that is considered as comprehensive and rigorous as that of a medical doctor. [3]

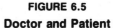

FIGURE 6.5
Doctor and Patient

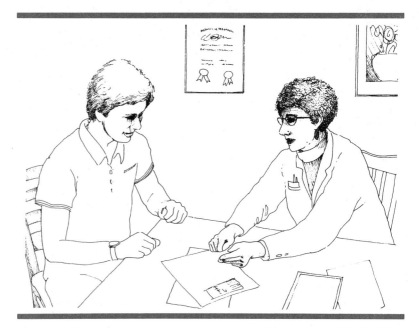

When discussing a health problem with your doctor, it is important to be specific about the symptoms you are experiencing. Be prepared to describe the nature of any pain or discomfort, the length of time you have been experiencing the symptoms, what brings them on, and whether you are currently taking any medications. It may be helpful to keep notes and write down any questions you have before you arrive at your appointment.

PLAN OF ACTION

Making choices that bring greater health and fitness yields its own rewards. Perhaps most important, it also makes possible the ability to enjoy life to the fullest and to give to life our best.

You may be wondering where the life-style changes discussed above fit into your daily and weekly routines. Below are some guidelines on where to start.

1. Have your overall goal in mind. You can arrive at your overall goal by assessing your current behavior or health level, determining what you would like your behavior or health level to be, and outlining benefits you wish to gain by

your new behavior or health level. Determine whether or not you feel highly motivated to attain this change for yourself.

2. Get a specific behavioral goal and draw up a detailed plan of action. This plan of action should include the day-to-day actions you plan to pursue. Determine whether or not you have at least an 80 percent chance of success in accomplishing this Action Plan on a regular basis.

3. Determine ways of keeping track of your progress. Identify the likely barriers you will face in following your plan of action and determine how you will cope with these barriers. Set dates on which you will assess your success.

4. Establish in advance a reward for following your plan of action and rewarding your success. ▧

Glossary

A

Acid rain: Rain that contains relatively high concentrations of acid-forming air pollutants such as sulfur and nitrogen oxides.

Acupuncture: A traditional Chinese health-care technique in which needles are inserted into specific points in the body in order to stimulate the release of endorphins, the body's natural painkillers.

Adrenal glands: A small, triangular shaped pair of glands located on top of the kidneys that secrete hormones including adrenaline (epinephrine) directly into the bloodstream.

Aerobic exercise: A form of exercise that increases respiration, intake of oxygen, heart rate, and cardiovascular fitness.

Allopathic medical care: The treatment of disease by using agents that produce effects different from those of the disease being treated.

Anorexia nervosa: An eating disorder characterized by refusal to eat that can lead to extreme loss of weight, hormonal disturbances, and even death.

Anxiety: An emotional state characterized by uneasiness, apprehension, or fear.

Asthma: An abrupt or chronic condition characterized by narrowed airways within the lungs that significantly obstruct airflow and cause difficulty in breathing.

Atherosclerosis: A form of hardening of the arteries in which a substance known as plaque gradually accumulates on artery walls, causing the blood vessels to lose elasticity and the arterial openings to narrow.

B

Biofeedback: A method of learning to control bodily functions by monitoring one's own muscle tension, skin temperature, and brain waves.

Blood lipid profile: A blood test administered to check the level of cholesterol and other fats in the blood.

C

Calcium: A silvery, metallic element that is the most abundant mineral in the body; an adequate supply of the calcium is essential for the growth and maintenance of the skeletal system and to a broad range of bodily functions; the main dietary sources of calcium are dairy products, eggs, green vegetables, fruit, and fish.

Carbon monoxide (CO): A colorless, odorless, and highly toxic gas formed as a by-product during the incomplete combustion of fossil fuels; it is also found in coal gas, the exhaust of internal combustion engines, and cigarette smoke.

Cardiologist: A medical doctor who specializes in the diagnosis and treatment of disorders involving the heart.

Cardiovascular disease: Any of several diseases of the heart and its blood vessels.

Catecholamines: Hormones, including adrenaline (epinephrine), that are released from the adrenal glands as part of the body's stress response; these substances serve to stimulate the body and prepare it for action.

Cerebrovascular disease: Injury to the brain through a thrombosis or clot in a blood vessel of the brain; also called a stroke.

Chemotherapy: Treatment involving the use of drugs or other medication designed to kill or reduce the growth rate of cancer cells.

Chiropractic: A method of treatment based primarily on the belief that the spinal column and nervous system interact and that, if adjustments to the spine can be made by external manipulation, relief from symptoms will occur.

Cholesterol: A fat-like substance found in animal foods and also manufactured by the body. Cholesterol is essential to nerve and brain cell function and to the synthesis of sex hormones and is also a component of bile acids used to aid fat digestion. It is also a part of atherosclerotic plaques that accumulate on artery walls (see "Coronary artery disease").

Chronic: Term used to describe any disorder that persists over a long period of time; in contrast to acute.

Circulatory system: The system consisting of the heart and blood vessels which maintains the flow of blood throughout the body.

Cirrhosis (of the liver): A disease that causes scarring and decreased functioning of the liver. It can be caused by chronic liver inflammation, hepatitis B, or chronic alcoholism.

Cocaine: A white, crystalline drug obtained from the leaves of the South American cocoa plant that produces feelings of euphoria and increased energy when absorbed into the bloodstream; continued use of cocaine can lead to psychological dependence.

Complex carbohydrate: A polysaccharide, or compound consisting of many sugar molecules linked together. Complex carbohydrates in the diet include starches and the fiber cellulose.

Consumerism: The movement that seeks to protect the rights of consumers against fraud, overcharging, unsafe or unhealthful products, and other abuses or damage caused by dishonest or careless business practices.

Coronary artery disease: Disease of the blood vessels near the heart in which the arteries become narrowed and clogged with raised patches known as atherosclerotic plaque. Atherosclerotic plaque consists of decaying muscle cells, fibrous tissue, clumps of blood platelets, cholesterol, lipoproteins, and sometimes calcium.

D

Deforestation: The deliberate or inadvertent removal of trees from the land resulting in a reduction of forest area.

Degenerative diseases: A general category encompassing a wide range of disorders involving progressive deterioration of the structure or ability to function of some portion of the body.

Depression: A mental state characterized by extreme sadness or dejection that persists for an extended period of time.

Diabetes: A disorder characterized by abnormally high levels of glucose (sugar) in the blood resulting from the failure of the pancreas to produce a sufficient supply of insulin, the hormone responsible for the conversion of glucose into a form usable by the cells of the body.

E

Ecosystem: A dynamic community that comprises all of the living creatures and their total environment within a specified area.

Endorphins: A group of substances formed within the body that relieves pain.

Epidemiological research: The study of large populations in order to investigate the causes and control of diseases.

Erysipelas: An infectious disorder of the face occurring primarily among children and the elderly that produces itchy red patches on the cheeks and nose followed by pimples that blister and then crust over; it is caused by streptococcal bacteria.

Esophagus: The tubular structure located immediately behind the windpipe (trachea) that connects the mouth and the stomach.

F

Fiber: Nondigestible residues of plant foods, primarily types of carbohydrates, some of which play a role in preserving the health of the gastrointestinal tract and lowering blood cholesterol.

G

Global warming: A gradual increase in the average annual temperature of the earth that some experts believe is currently underway and has the potential to cause many harmful effects.

H

HDL cholesterol: A lipid compound containing cholesterol removed from the arteries; also termed the "good" form of cholesterol because high levels are desirable and reduce the risk of heart disease.

Health spa: An often luxurious, residential, resort-like facility operated on a commercial basis that offers a variety of health-related services including weight-reduction programs.

Heart attack: The sudden death of part of the heart muscle. Also known as myocardial infarction.

Herbal medicine: A method of treatment that uses plant materials instead of human-fabricated medication to treat illness.

Holistic health: A view of health that encompasses the physiological, mental, emotional, social, spiritual, and environmental aspects of individuals and communities.

Homeopathy: A method of treatment that uses minute doses of drugs chosen as a cure because in a healthy person they produce symptoms that are similar to the disease being treated.

Hospice: A facility where care is provided to terminally ill individuals.

Hypertension: A chronic condition of high blood pressure, leading to increased risk for cardiovascular disease, stroke, and kidney disease.

I

Immune system: The body's natural defense system, which works to eliminate pathogens.

Immunization: The process of artificially bolstering the body's immunity against certain infectious diseases by the administration of a vaccine or other type of medication.

L

LDL cholesterol: A form of cholesterol that is deposited in the walls of arteries, contributing to the process of atherosclerosis. It is increased by overconsumption of saturated fat and cholesterol and contributes to the risk of heart disease.

Life expectancy: The estimated number of years of life remaining to a living organism, usually determined by comparing the organism's current age to the average age at death of other members of the species during some fixed period.

Life-style: A style of living that consistently reflects a particular set of values and attitudes.

Living will: A statement of personal instructions outlining the measures of heroic medical care (particularly life-support systems) desired and not desired by an individual, should that individual become incapacitated and unable to make decisions.

M

Marijuana: The dried flower clusters and leaves of the Indian hemp plant that, when smoked or consumed, produce a euphoric alteration of mood.

Melanoma: A skin cancer originating in the pigment-secreting cells of the skin that is highly malignant and may cause death.

Menopause: The cessation of menstruation in the female, typically between the ages of 45 and 50.

Metabolism: The chemical and physical processes inside living cells comprising the building up of new and the breaking down of old substances and tissues. Energy is released in the process.

Morphine: An opium derivative that relieves pain while producing a euphoric state; prolonged use can lead to dependence.

Mortality rate: The number of individual deaths occurring in a given population or group, usually expressed in relation to some baseline figure as in deaths per 100,000.

N

Narcotic: Any drug that dulls the senses or induces sleep and may produce dependence if used for a prolonged interval, especially the class of drugs derived from the opium poppy.

Nicotine: A poisonous alkaloid that is the chief psychoactive ingredient of tobacco.

Nutrition: The process by which we obtain the essential nutrients our bodies need to function.

O

Obesity: The excessive accumulation of fat in the body to a level that, depending on the age, frame size, and height of the affected person, is considered undesirable.

Opiate: Any drug derived from or chemically similar to opium, a drug prepared from the unripened pods of the opium poppy; a narcotic.

Osteopathic medicine: A system of diagnosis and treatment that recognizes the role of the collective musculoskeletal system (bones, muscles, tendons, tissues, nerves, and the spinal column) in the effective treatment of diseases and/or their symptoms.

Osteoporosis: Increased porosity of the bones, leading to weakness and a greater likelihood of fractures.

Ozone: A rare, poisonous form of oxygen; ozone occurs naturally in the upper atmosphere where it absorbs harmful ultraviolet radiation from the sun; ozone is a harmful air pollutant at ground level, where it forms as a byproduct of a variety of manufacturing processes and types of combustion.

P

Pancreas: A long, tapered, irregularly shaped gland behind the stomach that secretes a variety of digestive enzymes and hormones including insulin, which regulates the level of glucose (sugar) in the blood.

Pap smear: A test designed to detect abnormal changes in a small sample containing cells from the surface of the cervix (the neck of the uterus) thus preventing cervical cancer.

Pathologist: A person who studies disease, particularly its causes, processes, and effects on the body.

Pituitary gland: A small, pea-sized gland located at the base of the brain that regulates and controls the activity of the other endocrine glands (glands that release hormones directly into the bloodstream).

Placebo: A chemically inert substance administered in place of a drug. The benefit gained from taking a placebo occurs because the patient believes it will have a positive effect.

Premature death: Death before an individual reaches the standard life expectancy.

R

Resting heart rate: The heart rate (beats per minute) while an individual is completely at rest, most accurately determined while still lying down following a night's sleep.

Risk factor: A situation or condition that contributes to the likelihood that an undesirable outcome will occur, generally established by multiple scientific studies.

Risk-benefit analysis: A technique for assessing the likely outcome of a particular decision by quantifying and then comparing both the potential risks (losses) and benefits (gains).

S

Saturated fat: Organic acids containing carbon, oxygen, and the maximum quantity of hydrogen possible, combined with an oily alcohol called glycerol. Palm oil, coconut oil, and most animal fats are highly saturated.

Sedentary: Accustomed to sitting or being inactive.

Sidestream smoke: The smoke that escapes from the tip of the cigarette without being inhaled by the smoker.

Social support: The psychological, emotional, and other forms of support provided by spouse, family members, relatives, friends, acquaintances, and community ties.

Sodium: A mineral that helps regulate the body's water balance, maintain normal heart rhythm, and is vital to the transmission of impulses by the nervous system; the best known source of dietary sodium is sodium chloride (NaCl), table salt.

Stereotype: A popular but oversimplified and inaccurate perception or belief.

Stress: Any external stimulus, whether physical or psychological, that necessitates resistance, change, or adaptation by the individual.

Stroke: Damage to part of the brain caused by interruption in its blood supply, resulting in physical or mental impairment or even death.

T

Thrombosis: Coagulation of the blood into a clot that impedes circulation.

Toxic: Term used to describe any substance known to produce harmful or poisonous effects upon exposure, usually through interference with one or more of the basic chemical reactions that take place in living tissues.

Training zone: A range of heart rates (beats per minute) that effectively promotes cardiovascular fitness during exercise, generally defined as between 60 and 85 percent of an individual's maximum heart rate.

Trauma: Any sudden, severe, physical injury or psychological shock.

U

Ultraviolet rays: Light rays whose wavelength is less than that of the shortest visible light yet longer than that of X rays; prolonged exposure to ultraviolet light is potentially harmful.

W

Wellness: An approach to personal health that emphasizes individual responsibility for well-being through the practice of health-promoting life-style behaviors.

Y

Yoga: A system of exercises originating with the Hindu religion designed to promote control of the body and mind.

Notes

CHAPTER 1

1. Department of Health, Education and Welfare, *Healthy People: The Surgeon General's Report on Health Promotion and Disease Prevention—Background Papers* (Washington, DC: Government Printing Office, 1979).
2. David Brand, "A Nation of Healthy Worrywarts," *Time*, 25 July 1988, 66–67.
3. Brand, pp. 66–67.
4. Bernice Kanner, "Sin, You Eaters!" *New York* magazine, 10 April 1989, 28–30.
5. "How Americans make food choices: Results of a Gallup poll," *American Dietetic Association Courier* 29, no. 3 (1990): 2.
6. *American Dietetic Association Courier*, p. 2.
7. Kanner, p. 28.
8. Donald Vickery, M.D., *Life Plan for Your Health* (Reading, MA: Addison Wesley Publishing Co., 1978), 17–24.
9. Leonard Sagan, *The Health of Nations* (New York: Basic Books, Inc., 1987).
10. Sagan, p. 64.
11. Department of Health and Human Services, Public Health Service, Office of Disease Prevention and Health Promotion, *The 1990 Health Objectives of the Nation: A Midcourse Review* (Washington, DC: Government Printing Office, 1986), 15.
12. Vickery, p. 11.
13. Vickery, p. 14.
14. Vickery, p. 15.
15. Department of Health, Education and Welfare.

CHAPTER 2

1. Department of Health, Education and Welfare.
2. Department of Health, Education and Welfare.
3. Public Health Service, "Integration of Risk Factor Interventions," *The 1990 Health Objectives of the Nation: A Midcourse Review.*
4. Department of Health, Education and Welfare.
5. American Cancer Society, *Cancer Facts and Figures 1990*, (1989), 3.
6. Joint National Committee on Detection, Evaluation, and Treatment of High Blood Pressure, *The 1984 Report of the Joint*

National Committee on Detection, Evaluation, and Treatment of High Blood Pressure (Archives of Internal Medicine, 1984), 144, 1045–1057.

7. American Heart Association, *Heart Facts* (1985).

8. Committee on Diet and Health, Food and Nutrition Board, Commission on Life Sciences, National Research Council, "Dietary Intake and Nutritional Status: Trends and Assessment," *Diet and Health: Implications for Reducing Chronic Disease Risk* (Washington, DC: National Academy Press, 1989).

9. "Exercise and Heart Disease: the Smoking Gun," *University of California, Berkeley Wellness Letter* 4, no. 1 (October 1987): 1.

10. Committee on Diet and Health, pp. 16, 114–115.

11. "Safety: Holiday Driving," *University of California, Berkeley Wellness Letter* 2, no. 2 (December 1985): 8.

12. "Fascinating Facts," *University of California, Berkeley Wellness Letter* 6, no. 1 (October 1989): 1.

13. "Friendly Fire," *University of California, Berkeley Wellness Letter* 2, no. 11 (August 1986): 1.

14. "17 Tips for the Savvy Cyclist," *University of California, Berkeley Wellness Letter* 6, no. 9 (June 1990): 6.

15. "Remarkable Progress," *University of California, Berkeley Wellness Letter* 6, no. 2 (November 1989): 7.

16. "Fascinating Facts," *University of California, Berkeley Wellness Letter* 6, no. 3 (December 1989): 1.

17. "Remarkable Progress," *University of California, Berkeley Wellness Letter* 6, no. 2 (November 1989): 7.

18. "Fascinating Facts," *University of California, Berkeley Wellness Letter* 6, no. 3 (December 1989): 1.

19. "Fascinating Facts," *University of California, Berkeley Wellness Letter* 5, no. 9 (June 1989): 1.

20. "Fascinating Facts," *University of California, Berkeley Wellness Letter* 5, no. 10 (July 1989): 1.

21. "Fascinating Facts," *University of California, Berkeley Wellness Letter* 6, no. 1 (October 1989): 1.

22. Committee on Diet and Health.

23. "Fascinating Facts," *University of California, Berkeley Wellness Letter* 5, no. 9 (June 1989): 1.

24. L. Berkman and L. Breslow, *Health and Ways of Living: The Alameda County Study* (New York: Oxford University Press, 1983).

25. It is debatable whether eating 3 square meals a day and not snacking between meals increases longevity or has a positive effect on health. For a contrasting example, see the box

entitled "Eating on the Run: Eat Often and Plan Ahead," in chapter 4.

26. N. Belloc and L. Breslow, "Relationship of Physical Health and Health Practices," *Preventive Medicine* 1, no. 3 (1972): 409–421.

27. *Journal of the American Medical Association*, November 1989.

28. R. Paffenbarger et al., "Physical Activity, All-Cause Mortality, and Longevity of College Alumni," *New England Journal of Medicine*, 1986.

29. M. Sacks, "Mental Health and Physical Activity," *Contemporary Obstetrics and Gynecology*: 180–188.

CHAPTER 3

1. *Closing the Gap: The Burden of Unnecessary Illness,* Robert W. Amler and H. Bruce Dull, eds. (New York: Oxford University Press, 1987), 43.

2. Elliot J. Howard, M.D., *Health Risks* (Tucson, AZ: The Body Press, 1986), 21.

3. American Heart Association, *Silent Epidemic: The Truth About Women and Heart Disease* (1989), 6.

4. Howard, p. 32.

5. Howard, p. 33.

6. Howard, p. 29.

7. Howard, pp. 42–43.

8. "Exercise and Heart Disease: The Smoking Gun," *University of California, Berkeley Wellness Letter* 4, no. 1 (October 1987): 1.

9. Howard, p. 86.

10. Howard, p. 86.

11. D. Sandler et al., "Deaths from All Causes in Non-Smokers Who Lived with Smokers," *American Journal of Public Health* 79, no. 2 (1989): 163–167.

12. Howard, p. 93.

13. Paffenbarger et al.

14. Public Health Service, p. 15.

15. "Is It Necessary to Cut Down on Salt After All?" *Tufts University Diet and Nutrition Letter* 6, no. 6 (1988): 1.

16. Committee on Diet and Health, pp. 3–23.

17. Howard, p. 13.

18. "Over 50? Chances are you need more vitamin D," *Tufts University Diet and Nutrition Letter* 8, no. 4 (1990): 2.

19. Howard, pp. 140–141.

20. J. C. Quick and J. D. Quick, *Organizational Stress and Preventive Management* (New York: McGraw-Hill, 1984).

21. J. S. J. Manuso, "Stress Management and Behavioral Medicine: A Corporate Model," in *Health Promotion in the Workplace,* M. O'Donnell and T. Ainsworth, eds. (New York: John Wiley, 1982).
22. Public Health Service, pp. 128–129, and Vickery, pp. 146–147.

CHAPTER 4

1. S. Donoghue, "The Correlation Between Physical Fitness, Absenteeism and Work Performance," *Canadian Journal of Public Health* 68 (1977), 201–203.
2. "ACSM Guidelines for Fitness Updated," *Running and FitNews* 8, no. 7 (American Running and Fitness Association, 1990), 1.
3. Vickery, p. 106.
4. Vickery, p. 105.
5. *Journal of the American Geriatric Society* 37, no. 4 : 354–358.
6. Gary A. Klug and Janice Lettunich, *Wellness: Exercise & Physical Fitness* (Guilford, CT: The Dushkin Publishing Group, 1992).
7. Committee on Diet and Health.
8. Committee on Diet and Health.
9. Robert Garrison, Jr., and Elizabeth Somer, *The Nutrition Desk Reference* (New Canaan, CT: Keats Publishing, 1987), 118.
10. Judith Swarth, *Wellness: Nutrition & Health* (Guilford, CT: The Dushkin Publishing Group, 1992).
11. A. Chenault, *Nutrition and Health* (New York: Holt, Rinehart and Winston, 1984), 165–166.
12. Howard, pp. 149–150.
13. Randall R. Cottrell, *Wellness: Stress Management* (Guilford, CT: The Dushkin Publishing Group, 1992).
14. For further information on smoking and health, see Richard G. Schlaadt, *Wellness: Tobacco & Health* (Guilford, CT: The Dushkin Publishing Group, 1992).
15. Donald Kemper, Jim Giuffre, and Gene Drabinski, *Pathways Handbook: Success: Guide for a Healthy Life* (Boise, ID: Healthwise, Inc., 1986), 128.
16. Kemper, Giuffre, and Drabinski, p. 128.
17. For further information on this topic, see Richard G. Schlaadt, *Wellness: Alcohol Use & Abuse* (Guilford, CT: The Dushkin Publishing Group, 1992).
18. "Pain Relief," *University of California, Berkeley Wellness Letter* 5, no. 11 (August 1989): 4–5.

19. "Marijuana: What We Know," *University of California, Berkeley Wellness Letter* 6, no. 6 (March 1990): 2–3.

20. Vickery, p. 156.

21. Mark Tager and Jeffrey Harris, *Improving Your Odds: A Planning Guide for High-Level Health* (Beaverton, OR: Great Performance, Inc., 1986), 34.

22. Richard G. Schlaadt, *Wellness: Drugs, Society & Behavior* (Guilford, CT: The Dushkin Publishing Group, 1992).

23. Vickery, p. 148.

24. "Pain Relief," *University of California, Berkeley Wellness Letter* 5, no. 11 (August 1989): 4–5.

25. "Moving to an Upbeat," *University of California, Berkeley Wellness Letter* 2, no. 11 (August 1986): 1.

26. Andrew Weil, M.D., *Health and Healing: Understanding Conventional and Alternative Medicine* (Boston: Houghton Mifflin, 1983).

27. "Laughing Toward Longevity," *University of California, Berkeley Wellness Letter* 1, no. 9 (1985): 1.

28. Sagan, p. 116.

29. Ivan Illich, *Medical Nemesis: The Expropriation of Health* (New York: Pantheon Books, 1976).

30. "Overcoming the Wintertime Blahs," *University of California, Berkeley Wellness Letter* 2, no. 2 (December 1985): 1.

31. Mark Tager and Marjorie Blanchard, *Working Well* (New York: Simon and Schuster, 1985), 52–53.

CHAPTER 5

1. L. Berkman and S. Syme, "Assessing the Physical Health Effects of Social Networks and Social Support," *Annual Review of Public Health* 5 (1984): 413–432.

2. G. Comstock and K. Partridge, "Church Attendance and Health," *Journal of Chronic Diseases* 25 (1972): 665–672.

3. G. W. Brown, and T. O. Harris, *Social Origins of Depression* (New York: Free Press, 1978), and Sagan.

4. T. Drabek and W. Key, *Conquering Disaster: Family Recovery and Long-Term Consequences* (New York: Irvington, 1984).

5. B. MacMahon and T. Pugh, *Epidemiology: Principles and Methods* (Boston: Little, Brown and Co., 1970).

6. C. Darcy and C. Siddique, "Marital Status and Psychological Well-Being: A Cross-National Comparative Analysis," *International Journal of Comparative Sociology* 26 (1986): 146–166.

7. Sagan, p. 32, and S. Minuchin, B. Rosman, and L. Baker, *Psychosomatic Families* (Cambridge, MA: Harvard University Press, 1978).

8. E. Friedman et al., "Animal Companions: One-Year Survival after Discharge from a Coronary Care Unit," *Public Health Reports* 95 (1980): 307–312, and L. Bustad, *Animals, Aging and the Aged* (Minneapolis, MN: University of Minnesota Press, 1980), and *Interrelations Between People and Animals*, B. Fogel, ed. (Springfield, IL: Charles C. Thomas, 1981).

9. F. Kasch et al., *The Physician and Sportsmedicine* 16, no. 1 (1988): 117–125.

10. N. Belloc and L. Breslow, "Relationship of Physical Health and Health Practices," *Preventive Medicine* 1, no. 3 (1972): 409–421.

11. For further information on this topic, see James D. Porterfield and Richard St. Pierre, *Wellness: Healthful Aging* (Guilford, CT: The Dushkin Publishing Group, 1992).

12. "When to Turn the Electricity Off," *University of California, Berkeley Wellness Letter* 5, no. 3 (December 1988): 2.

13. "The TV Set," *Self* magazine, June 1990, 69.

14. "Videobesity," *University of California, Berkeley Wellness Letter* 6, no. 8 (May 1990): 6.

15. "Videobesity," *University of California, Berkeley Wellness Letter* 6, no. 8 (May 1990): 6.

16. See, for example, the more recent EPA study, "EPA Says Pesticides, Nitrates Taint Hundreds of Communities' Drinking Water," the Baltimore *Sun,* 14 November 1990, 11A.

CHAPTER 6

1. For additional information on how to become a better health consumer, see the following volume from this series: Robert E. Kime, *Wellness: The Informed Health Consumer* (Guilford, CT: The Dushkin Publishing Group, 1992).

2. A particularly useful source of additional information on allopathic and alternative medicine is Andrew Weil's *Health and Healing: Understanding Conventional and Alternative Medicine,* listed in Resources section at end of this volume.

3. Nadine Stair of Louisville, Kentucky, cited in Gordon Edlin and Eric Golanty, *Health and Wellness* (Boston: Science Books International, 1982).

Resources

BOOKS

Anderson, Bob. *Stretching*. New York: Random House, 1980.

A useful book shows the correct way to stretch for fitness and muscle flexibility. More than 200 stretches and stretching routines for 36 different sports and activities are illustrated with over 1,000 drawings.

Bailey, Covert. *Fit or Fat Target Diet*. Boston: Houghton Mifflin, 1984.

This easy-to-read, often humorous book, makes important points about exercise and diet. It encourages the reader to maintain a regular aerobic exercise program, and explains why dieting alone is not the answer to controlling weight. The author maintains that all the vitamins and minerals the average healthy person needs can be obtained by eating the right foods, without need for supplements. Bailey's target diet focuses on eating a balanced diet from all the major food groups and eating foods low in fat, low in sugar, and high in fiber.

Brody, Jane. *Jane Brody's Nutrition Book*. New York: Bantam Books, 1987.

A comprehensive guide by the health journalist at the *New York Times* covering nutrients, nutrition guidelines, nutrition and disease, weight management, food labeling, and the special needs of athletes, pregnant women, children, adolescents, the elderly, and vegetarians. The author explains the benefits of good eating and how to make sensible dietary changes.

Brody, Jane. *The New York Times Guide to Personal Health*. New York: The New York Times Book Co., 1982.

Based on Jane Brody's award-winning and immensely popular "Personal Health" columns from the *New York Times*, this book helps the reader take charge of his or her health. It teaches how to stay healthy, how to participate in medical care, what to do when things go wrong, how to avoid unnecessary and expensive treatment, and how to get better care from doctors. Fifteen sections cover: nutrition, exercise, emotional health, environmental health effects, common serious illness, and more.

Brown, Lester R. *The State of the World 1990*. New York: W. W. Norton, 1990.

This annually-published report summarizes issues affecting the world environment: sustainable agriculture, hunger, waste disposal, water supply and safety, transportation, land degradation, ozone destruction, and other critical issues. This book provides an excellent overview of issues for those concerned about environmental links to health and wellness.

Burstein, Nancy. *Soft Aerobics: The New Low-Impact Workout*. New York: Putnam, 1987.

This book presents an alternative to traditional, high-impact aerobics (which can cause injury from excess stress on ankles, shins, calves, knees, hips, and back). Twelve low-impact exercises combined into 4 different exercise routines are presented. Illustrated with step-by-step photographs. Readers can follow the specific routines presented in the book, or create a personalized program for individual fitness levels. The program is effective for losing weight as well as preventing osteoporosis in women.

Clayman, Charles B., ed. *The American Medical Association Home Medical Encyclopedia*. 2 vols. New York: Random House, 1989.

A guide designed to answer numerous medical questions, including the causes, symptoms, diagnosis, and treatment of communicable diseases such as Lyme Disease, sexually transmitted disease (STD), bacterial and viral infections, and so on. The book is arranged alphabetically by subject for quick reference.

Connor, Sonja L., M.S., and William E. Connor, M.D. *The New American Diet: The Lifetime Family Eating Plan for Good Health*. New York: Simon & Schuster, 1986.

An eating guide for families that emphasizes gradual change into healthier eating habits, particularly lower fat intake. The diet is divided into three phases. Phase One focuses on the modification of recipes and eating habits. Phase Two begins to lower meat consumption and present new recipes. Phase Three incorporates beans and grains as the main protein sources, rather than higher-fat meat sources.

Cooper, Kenneth H. *Controlling Cholesterol: Dr. Kenneth H. Cooper's Preventive Medicine Program*. New York: Bantam, 1988.

The author presents a program for identifying and reducing personal risk of heart disease and for controlling cholesterol levels. Also discussed are diet, alcohol, smoking, exercise, stress, birth control pills, fish oil, fiber, how to obtain an accurate blood-cholesterol profile, and other topics.

Franks, B. Don, and Edward T. Howley. *Fitness Facts: The Healthy Living Handbook*. Champaign, IL: Human Kinetics Publishers, 1989.

Discussed in this book are how to test fitness, improve fitness level, and set up an individual fitness program based on current research. The authors answer many basic questions about exercise and fitness. Chapters contain: fitness progress self-evaluation, definitions of fitness, how to change to more healthful behaviors, selecting the right fitness program, injury prevention, and more.

Griffith, H. Winter, M.D. *Complete Guide to Medical Tests*. Tucson, AZ: Fisher Books, 1988.

Explained in this book are 450 common tests, factors that influence these tests (such as diet, medications, and alcohol), costs, equipment used, and how long a particular test takes. Also explained are the sensations you will feel, hear, see, smell, and taste during these tests, normal test values, and post-test care.

Griffith, H. Winter, M.D. *Complete Guide to Prescription and Non-Prescription Drugs: Side Effects, Warnings, and Vital Data For Safe Use*. rev. ed. Tucson, AZ: HP Books, 1990.

This book covers over 5,000 brand names and 550 generic medications, including dosage and usage information of each drug, their side effects, and interactions with other drugs and foods. Also included is information on what to do in case of an overdose.

Griffith, H. Winter, M.D. *Complete Guide to Vitamins: Vitamins and Supplements*. Tucson, AZ: Fisher Books, 1988.

This book provides easy-to-read charts covering over 75 vitamins, minerals, nucleic and amino acids, and other supplements. Also provides information on commonly used medicinal herbs. These charts show deficiency symptoms, RDA recommendations, warnings and precautions for use, signs of overdose, adverse reactions and side effects, and possible interactions with drugs and other substances.

Guide to More Healthful Living. Edited by the Blue Cross/Blue Shield Association. New York: Contemporary Books, 1986.

A book that covers overall wellness of body and mind. Written and compiled by nine medical doctors, chapter titles include "Wellness," "Nutrition," "Physical Fitness," "Reducing Stress," and "Your Health and Fitness Lifestyle." Two additional sections include Your Healthy Best Score Card, which allows you to chart your health progress, and The Life Management Self-Evaluation Test, which includes questions about eating habits, physical activity, environment, smoking habits, and stress evaluations, all culminating in your own total Life Management score.

Howard, Elliot J., M.D., with Susan A. Roth. *Health Risks*. Tuscon, AZ: The Body Press, 1986.

This book provides a detailed discussion of the risk factors and life-style changes that reduce the likelihood of developing cancer, heart disease, stroke, osteoporosis, diabetes, and stress-related problems.

Keet, Robert B., M.D., and Mary Nelson, M.S. *The Medical Marketplace*. Santa Cruz, CA: Network Publications, 1985.

Presented in this book are information and checklists to help you plan your health care and make health decisions. Covers choosing a physician, emergency care, medications, surgery, and other topics.

Kunz, Jeffery R. M., and Asher J. Finkel, M.D., eds. *The American Medical Association Family Medical Guide*. New York: Random House, 1987.

This comprehensive guide covers topics ranging from maintaining a healthy body to caring for the ill. A section on symptoms and self-diagnosis uses flow charts to help the reader track down the possible significance of a particular symptom or set of symptoms, and another section provides explanations of diseases and disorders.

McGuire, Meredith B. *Ritual Healing in Suburban America*. New Brunswick, NJ: Rutgers University Press, 1988.

This book examines the nature of spiritual healing as a method that many well-educated, middle-class people use to combat ailments that conventional health care often ignores. The book shows that alternative healing systems are very diverse, but fall roughly into five broad types: Christian healing, Eastern meditation and human-potential groups, traditional metaphysical groups, psychic and occult groups, and manipulation/technique practitioners. All view health, illness and healing with a different perspective than the main biological focus of modern medicine.

Meyers, Casey. *Aerobic Walking: The Best and Safest Weight Loss and Cardiovascular Exercise for Everyone Overweight or Out of Shape.* New York: Random House, 1987.

This book addresses the benefits of walking for the purpose of disease prevention and helping with weight-control problems. Covered are the proper walking gaits for maximum aerobic benefits and reduced stress on joints and how to develop a self-tailored fitness walking program.

The New Illustrated Family Medical and Health Guide. By the Editors of Consumer's Guide. Lincolnwood, IL: Publications International, 1991.

This book covers a wide variety of health and medical topics, to help readers make the best decisions about personal and family health-care needs. It provides information to help choose the right doctor, stay healthy, prevent illness, and to be better informed on medical and health-care systems, tests, and treatments. Also included are nutrition and life-style guidelines and sections on recognizing and coping with common symptoms, infectious diseases, and inherited conditions.

Robertson, Laurel, Carol Flinders, and Brian Ruppenthal. *The New Laurel's Kitchen.* 2d ed. Berkeley, CA: Ten Speed Press, 1986.

A cookbook and nutrition handbook for vegetarians and those interested in reducing meat or fat intake. Contains over 150 vegetarian recipes and extensive tables showing the nutritional composition of each food used in the recipes. A review of nutritional guidelines for vegetarians provides accurate, useful background information.

Shlian, Joel N., M.D., and Deborah M. Shlian. *Self-Help Handbook: Of Symptoms and Treatments.* Contemporary Books: New York, 1986.

This book is provided by the Blue Cross/Blue Shield Association, and is intended as a symptom-oriented consumer health guide. Sections include: Keys to Good Health, which covers doctor selection and ways to protect your health and reduce risks to health; Symptoms Affecting the Entire Body; Symptoms and Disease Affecting Specific Body Systems; Symptoms and Disease of Children; and Common Medical Emergencies. The chapters indicate the steps to take to protect your health when problems arise.

Tribole, Evelyn, M.S., R.D. *Eating on the Run.* Champaign, IL: Life Enhancement Publications, 1987.

A helpful handbook that shows how to work a balanced diet into a busy schedule. Includes guidelines for choosing in fast-food restaurants, selecting frozen convenience foods, and preparing quick meals in 60 minutes or less. The author also discusses weight-control techniques and meal and snack planning strategies, and provides 24 quick recipes and nutrition content charts.

NEWSLETTERS

ACSH News and Views is published five times a year by the American Council on Science and Health, a nonprofit educational association. The newsletter discusses topics related to food, chemicals, the environment, and health. A one-year subscription is $15. Write to ACSH News and Views, 1995 Broadway, New York, NY 10023, or call (212) 362-7044.

Consumer Reports Health Letter is published monthly by Consumers Union of the United States, a nonprofit organization that provides information and advice on goods, services, health and personal finance. A one-year subscription is $24, and two years cost $38. Write to the Subscription Director, Consumer Reports Health Letter, Box 56356, Boulder, CO 80322-6356, or call (800) 274-8370.

Environmental Nutrition: The Professional Newsletter of Diet, Nutrition and Health is an interesting monthly publication featuring informative and reliable articles on diet and nutrition. A one-year subscription is $36. Write to Environmental Nutrition, 2112 Broadway, New York, NY 10023.

Harvard Health Letter is published monthly as a nonprofit service by the Department of Continuing Education, Harvard Medical School, in association with Harvard University Press. The letter has the goal of interpreting health information for general readers in a timely and accurate fashion. A one-year subscription is $21. Write to the Harvard Medical School Letter, 79 Garden Street, Cambridge, MA 02138, or call customer service at (617) 495-3975.

Healthline is published monthly by Healthline Publishing, Inc. The letter is intended to educate readers about ways to help themselves avoid illness and live longer, healthier lives. A one-year subscription is $19, or $34 for two years. Write to Healthline, The C. V. Mosby Company, 11830 Westline Industrial Drive, St. Louis, MO 63146-3318, or call (800) 325-4177 (ext. 351).

Johns Hopkins Medical Letter, Health After 50 is published monthly by Medletter Associates, Inc., and covers a variety of topics related to healthful living. A one-year subscription is $20. Write to the Johns Hopkins Medical Letter, P.O. Box 420179, Palm Coast, FL 32142.

Lahey Clinic Health Letter is published monthly to bring readers timely, relevant information about important medical issues. Continuing topics include: general healthfulness, natural and processed foods, depression, exercise, alcohol, prescription medicine therapy, major diseases, and exercise. A one-year subscription is $18. Write to the Lahey Clinic Health Letter, Subscription Department, P.O. Box 541, Burlington, MA 01805.

Mayo Clinic Nutrition Letter is published monthly and provides reliable information about nutrition and fitness and how decisions on these matters affect your health. A one-year subscription is $24. Write to the Mayo Foundation for Medical Education and Research, 200 1st Street SW, Rochester, MN 55905, or call (800) 888-3968.

Running & FitNews is published monthly by the American Running and Fitness Association, a nonprofit educational association of athletes and sports medicine professionals. This newsletter provides information on exercise guidelines, injuries, diet, and health-related fitness topics. A one-year subscription is $25. Write to the AR&FA, 9310 Old Georgetown Road, Bethesda, MD 20814, or call (301) 897-0197.

Tufts University Diet and Nutrition Letter is published monthly and covers topics related to nutrition and wellness, including exercise, diet and disease, and food consumerism. A one-year subscription costs $20. Write to the Tufts University Diet and Nutrition Letter, 53 Park Place, New York, NY 10007.

University of California Berkeley Wellness Letter is published monthly and covers many topics, including nutrition, fitness, and stress management. A one-year subscription is $20. Write to the University of California, Berkeley Wellness Letter, P.O. Box 420148, Palm Coast, FL 32142.

PERIODICALS

American Health Magazine: Fitness of Body and Mind is published 10 times a year and covers every aspect of physical and mental well-being. In addition to feature articles, ongoing departments include Nutrition News, Fitness Reports, Mind/Body News, Family Report, Family Pet, and more. A one-year subscription is $14.95. Write to American Health: Fitness of Body and Mind, P.O. Box 3015, Harlan, IA 51537-3015.

Cooking Light Magazine is published 6 times a year. Developed by nutritionists and dieticians, this colorful magazine provides a wealth of information on cooking with less fat and sugar, and contains interesting food and nutrition articles, practical meal planning information, and creative recipes with amounts of fat, cholesterol, sodium, and calories per serving provided. A one-year subscription is $12. Write to Cooking Light, P.O. Box C-549, Birmingham, AL 35283.

Health Magazine is published 10 times a year by Family Media, Inc. This magazine features a half-dozen articles per issue on fitness for both mind and body, environmental topics, sporting activities, health, and food. It has a regular Healthline section dealing with topics related to behavior, medical information, and children's health. A one-year subscription is $19.95. Write to Health Magazine, Subscription Dept., P.O. Box 420030, Palm Coast, FL 32142-0030, or call (800) 423-1780; in Florida (800) 858-0095.

In Health Magazine is published 6 times a year and provides articles on a number of health issues. In addition to recipes and practical nutrition tips, the magazine regularly includes self-help resources for consumers. A one-year subscription is $18. Write to In Health, P.O. Box 52431, Boulder, CO 80321-2431.

Priorities: For Long Life & Good Health is published quarterly by the American Council of Science and Health, Inc. (ACSH), a nonprofit consumer education association concerned with nutrition, chemicals, life-style factors, the environment, and human health. General individual membership in ACSH, which includes a subscription to *Priorities*, costs $25 a year. Write to the Subscription Department, Priorities, 1995 Broadway, 16th Floor, New York, NY 10023-5860.

HOTLINES

American Diabetes Association, (800) ADA-DISC. Staff members will answer general questions about diabetes, risk factors, and symptoms. Free literature, and a free quarterly newsletter, *Diabetes '91*, will be sent upon request. Service available 8:30 A.M. to 5:00 P.M., Eastern Standard Time, Monday through Friday.

American Dietetic Association, (800) 877-1600. The American Dietetic Association (ADA) is the major professional organization for the dietetic profession. The ADA will answer questions and provide information to callers on subjects related to foods and nutrition.

Cancer Information Service, (800) 4-CANCER. This hotline is funded by the National Cancer Institute and staffed by professionals and volunteers. They will answer questions on causes of cancer, its prevention, detection, and treatment, and other cancer-related problems. Literature is available and referrals are made to cancer support groups, treatment facilities, and transportation services. Available 9.00 A.M. to 10.00 P.M., Monday through Friday and 10:00 A.M. to 6 P.M. Saturday, Eastern Standard Time.

National Health Information Center, Department of Health and Human Services, (800) 336-4797. Operated by the Office of Disease Prevention and Health Promotion, this information and referral center's trained personnel will direct you to the organization or government agency that can assist you with your health question, whether it's about high blood pressure, cancer, fitness, or any other topic. Available 9:00 A.M. to 5:00 P.M., Eastern Standard Time, Monday through Friday.

Tel-Med is a free telephone service provided in many cities. You can call and ask for a specific tape number, and have the health message played for you over the phone. There are over 300 medical topics to choose from, including topics related to maintaining a healthy life-style, and many states provide toll-free numbers for this service. Call your local information operator to find the nearest Tel-Med office, or write to Tel-Med, Box 970, Colton, CA 92324.

VIDEOTAPES

The following video programs related to wellness topics can be ordered from the National Wellness Institute, Inc., South Hall, 1319 Fremont Street, Stevens Point, WI 54481. Write for format, price, and ordering information.

Living With High Blood Pressure is hosted by Arthur Ashe, legendary tennis great and heart attack victim. This video will help you learn how heredity and life-style affect your blood pressure, how to understand the disease clearly, and how to live with high blood pressure.

Lower Your Cholesterol Now! is an upbeat, informative, and practical video. Dietician Leni Reed provides answers and advice on how to make wise nutritional choices to lower calories, saturated fat, and cholesterol in your diet.

Stanford Health and Exercise Program brings together fitness specialists and world-class athletes to introduce the concepts and practical tools found in the accompanying handbook, *The Stanford Health and Exercise Handbook*. Sections feature: eight prime benefits of exercise, determining your basic level of fitness, the actual Stanford Workout program, three low-impact aerobic workouts, and more.

Swing into Shape is a low-intensity nonaerobic exercise video for the aging population. It focuses on the improvement of muscle tone, strength, and flexibility. The three 26-minute routines are designed to acknowledge the physical limitations of this population. Designed by Betsy Bork, physical therapist.

The next four videos are available from Nutrition Counseling and Education Services (NC&ES), P.O. Box 3018, Olathe, KS 66062-3018. Write for prices and ordering information, or call (913) 782-8230. The following toll-free number is for placing orders only: (800) 445-5653. All videos in VHS format only.

Any Body Can Sit and Be Fit was commissioned by the Illinois State Medical Auxiliary for use in nursing homes by the wheelchair-bound or other individuals who find it difficult to stand and do exercise. Flexibility is improved by following the exercises in this 20-minute video.

Supermarket Savvy Tour Video by dietician Leni Reed takes you on a tour through a supermarket. Reed guides you through the aisles while instructing you in the art of label-reading. Shows how to make informed, healthier food choices and how to sort out the important information from the mumbo-jumbo. Very helpful for those concerned about cholesterol and fat.

Thin Dining shows how to choose restaurants, order assertively, and eat well in ethnic restaurants while minimizing calories. Also covered are choosing in fast-food restaurants and how to select airline meals.

Warming Up: The Gentle Exercise Videotape for Formerly Inactive People. This program is designed for people who want to start, or get back to, enjoying regular exercise for fun, healing, and health. Also useful to people who are overweight.

GOVERNMENT, CONSUMER AND ADVOCACY GROUPS

American Cancer Society (ACS), 1599 Cliffs Road, Atlanta, GA 30329, (404) 320-3333
  The ACS supports education and research in cancer prevention, diagnosis, detection, and treatment, including the health effects of smoking. Provides special services to cancer patients. Sponsors Reach to Recovery, CanSurmount, and I Can Cope.

American Health Foundation (AHF), 320 East 43d Street, New York, NY 10017, (212) 953-1900
  Devoted to promoting preventive medicine. The Foundation conducts research into nutrition and environmental carcinogens, provides clinical research and services for adults and children, educates laypeople and medical personnel in the principles of preventive medicine, and investigates the costs of disease and compares them with the costs of preventive approaches. Publishes *Health Letter*, bi-monthly.

American Heart Association (AHA), 720 Greenville Avenue, Dallas, TX 75231, (214) 373-6300
  The AHA supports research, education, and community service programs with the goal of reducing premature death and disability from stroke and cardiovascular disease. It also publishes several books, periodicals, and pamphlets related to healthy heart management. State branches of the AHA can be located through directory information.

American Lung Association (ALA), 1740 Broadway, New York, NY 10019, (212) 315-8700
  Membership includes a federation of state and local associations of physicians, nurses, and laypeople interested in the prevention and control of lung disease. Works with other organizations in planning and conducting programs in community services; public, professional and patient education; and research. Makes policy recommendations regarding medical care of respiratory disease, occupational health, hazards of smoking, and air conservation. The ALA is financed by the annual Christmas Seal Campaign and other fund-raising activities.

American Medical Association (AMA), 515 North State Street, Chicago, IL 60610, (312) 464-5000 to get the operator, (312) 464-4446 to get the reference library.
  The AMA disseminates scientific information to members and the general public. Informs members on significant medical and health legislation on state and national levels, and represents the profession before Congress and government agencies. Ad hoc committees are formed for such topics as health-care planning and principles of medical ethics.

Center for Science in the Public Interest (CSPI), 1755 S Street, NW, Washington, DC 20009
  The CSPI monitors food manufacturers and federal agencies involved in food regulation, safety, and trade. They investigate and initiate legal actions against unsafe and unfair practices related to food and nutrition. They publish nutrition education materials and a newsletter covering nutrition and health, food regulation updates, and healthful cooking. *Nutrition Action* is published monthly.

Centers for Disease Control (CDC), Dr. Robert Waller, Project Coordinator, 1600 Cliffs Park, Executive Plaza, Building 26, Mail Stop E25, Atlanta, GA 30333, (404) 639-3311
  This main number goes to an operator who will then direct you toward the specific information laboratory for the disease for which you seek information, such as hepatitis, AIDS, various venereal diseases, and so on. You may also be referred to someone in the public inquiry department, who will in turn help direct your inquiry for a specific disease.

High Blood Pressure Information Center (HBPIC), 120/80 National Institutes of Health, Bethesda, MD 20205, (301) 652-7700
  The HBPIC provides information on the detection, diagnosis, and management of high blood pressure to consumers and health professionals. The center identifies, collects, organizes, and disseminates information in many formats. Its sources are monographs, journals,

newsletters, newspapers, reports, audiovisuals, brochures, posters, and contacts with other health agencies and clearinghouses. Also provides reference and referral services, consultants, a speaker's register, packets, searches on the center's data base and resources of other libraries and clearinghouses, and referrals to other sources.

National Association of Anorexia Nervosa and Associated Disorders (ANAD), Box 7, Highland Park, IL 60035, (312) 831-3438

Offers assistance to anorexics, bulimics, their families, and others interested in the problems of anorexia nervosa and bulimia. Maintains chapters in 45 states. Seeks better understanding of and prevention and cures for these eating disorders. Educates the public and health professionals on these illnesses and their treatments. Acts as a resource center, compiling and providing information. Works to end discrimination, and fights against the use of misleading advertising and the production, marketing, and distribution of dangerous diet aids.

President's Council on Physical Fitness and Sports, Washington, DC 20201, (202) 755-7478

The council conducts a public service advertising program and cooperates with governmental and private groups to promote the development of physical fitness leadership, facilities, and programs. Produces educational materials on exercise, school physical education programs, and sports and physical fitness for youth, adults, and the elderly. Most states have a chapter of this organization identified as the Governor's Council on Physical Fitness and Sports.

Index

CREDITS AND ACKNOWLEDGMENTS

Page 2 Table 1.1 Reprinted from *American Health Magazine*. Copyright © 1989. Page 4 Table 1.2 Reprinted from *American Health Magazine*. Copyright © 1989. Page 8 Table 1.5 Adapted from *LifePlan* by Donald M. Vickery, M.D. Copyright © 1990; available from Victor, Inc., 3661 Overlook Trail, Evergreen, CO 80439. Page 10 Table 1.6 Adapted from *Mortality and Morbidity Weekly Report* with permission, and William C. Cockerham, *Medical Sociology, 4th Edition*. Copyright © 1989, p. 29. Reprinted with permission of Prentice Hall, Englewood Cliffs, New Jersey. Page 11 Excerpted from *University of California, Berkeley Wellness Letter*. Reprinted by permission. Copyright © Health Letter Associates, 1990. Page 12 Reprinted from John W. Travis, *Wellness Workbook*. Copyright © 1977, 1981, 1988. Available from Wellness Associates, Box 5433-D, Mill Valley, CA 94942. Page 15 Reprinted with permission of *University of California, Berkeley Wellness Letter*. Copyright © Health Letter Associates, 1990. Page 18 Copyright © 1985, the *Washington Post*. Reprinted with permission. Page 23 Reprinted with permission of *University of California, Berkeley Wellness Letter*. Copyright © Health Letter Associates, 1990. Page 40 Reprinted with permission from the American Cancer Society *Guidelines to Reduce Risk for Cancer*. Copyright © 1985, American Cancer Society, Inc. Page 49 Copyright © the *San Francisco Chronicle*. Reprinted by permission. Page 53 Reprinted with permission of *University of California, Berkeley Wellness Letter*. Copyright © Health Letter Associates, 1990. Page 59 Reprinted with permission from *Environmental Nutrition Newsletter*, 2112 Broadway #200, New York, NY 10023. Page 62 Reprinted from *Running and FitNews*, 9310 Old Georgetown Rd., Bethesda, MD 20814. Page 65 Reprinted with permission from *Environmental Nutrition Newsletter*, 2112 Broadway #200, New York, NY 10023. Page 79 Reprinted with permission of *University of California, Berkeley Wellness Letter*. Copyright © Health Letter Associates, 1990. Page 84 Copyright © 1978 by Jane Howard. Reprinted by permission of Simon & Schuster, Inc. Page 86 Reprinted from Charles Jennings and Mark J. Tager, *Medical Self-Care*, Summer 1981. Page 89 Reprinted with permission of *University of California, Berkeley Wellness Letter*. Copyright © Health Letter Associates, 1990. Page 91 Reprinted with permission of *University of California, Berkeley Wellness Letter*. Copyright © Health Letter Associates, 1990. Page 95 Reprinted with permission of *University of California, Berkeley Wellness Letter*. Copyright © Health Letter Associates, 1990. Page 103 Reprinted from *American Health Magazine*. Copyright © 1990 by Joel Gurin. Page 108 Table 6.1 Reprinted from *American Health Magazine*. Copyright © 1990. Page 109 Table 6.2 Reprinted from *American Health Magazine*. Copyright © 1990.